SMOKE & MIRRORS

SMOKE & MIRRORS

THE INSIDE STORY OF TELEVISION NEWS IN CANADA

PETER TRUEMAN

McCLELLAND AND STEWART

The Canadian Publishers
McClelland and Stewart Limited
25 Hollinger Road
Toronto   M4B 3G2

Printed and bound in Canada
by John Deyell Company

CANADIAN CATALOGUING IN PUBLICATION DATA

Trueman, Peter, 1934-
  Smoke and mirrors

ISBN 0 7710 8613 X

1. Television broadcasting of news — Canada.
I. Title.

PN4914.T4T78   791.45'5   C80 094035-0

For my mother, Jean Miller Trueman,
and my father, Albert William Trueman

Contents

Preface

I'm not sure that when McClelland and Stewart agreed to a book on Canadian television news, they expected *Smoke and Mirrors*. The book is much more than an examination of the state of the industry, it is one man's clenched-fist salute to the crap merchants who dominate Canadian television, public and private. I am particularly critical of the CBC, not because it doesn't do the best programming in this country, but because it doesn't do enough of it, and because the good television it produces tends to be despite the CBC's management, not because of it. The serious programming on the two commercial networks, Global and CTV, is so nearly non-existent that it is hardly worthy of mention. And if the private networks redeem themselves at all, it is in news programming, where they do almost as much as the CBC, with a fraction of the CBC's budget.

I blame the people who own Canadian television for this state of affairs, because they have worried too much about the pocketbooks of their shareholders, and not enough about the minds of their viewers. I blame the Canadian Radio-Television and Telecommunications Commission (CRTC), for fussing about Canadian content instead of fuming about Canadian quality. I blame the politicians for meekly handing the CBC $430 million of the taxpayers' money each year, too much of it to support a gaggle of unproductive supernumeraries, too much of it to support the commercial portions of the CBC's schedule. And I blame the newspapers, who have failed to take television or television criticism seriously, and have thereby licenced a platoon of peevish dilettantes who can't seem to see the forest for the trees.

I have worked in news for three Canadian dailies and three television networks for almost a quarter of a century. This book represents what I have come to believe about broadcasting in general and television news in particular. It does not pretend to be a complete, unbiased, or dispassionate account. It is television news as I remember my own encounters with it, bolstered by material from my own reading on the subject and stacks of personal files containing ancient directives, speeches, and clippings, my own and others.

The book contains the kind of things I would talk about if I held a captive audience in a snow-bound cabin, and that audience showed the slightest interest in television news. The book is the letter I wish I could have written every time I received some thoughtful criticism from a viewer. It is also the speech I have tried to deliver every time I've sat tongue-tied in the office of Global's president, Paul Morton, trying to tell him what I feel about the direction of the industry.

You may have wondered about the title, *Smoke and Mirrors*. It may suggest that, like the magician, TV news tries to fool you. It's true that, like any would-be Blackstone, TV newsmen are in the business of selling illusions. And sometimes we do try to convince the viewer that the lady has been sawed in half when she is still safely in one piece. But the major illusion we try to peddle is that TV news is easy. I hope the book demonstrates that it isn't.

The title comes from a pet phrase of Bill Cunningham's, Global's vice-president of News. It's one he uses when we are about to embark on an assignment we hope will make our news service look bigger and better than it really is. I knew that using this phrase as a title would be a bit near the bone. The moment of truth came one evening last July, at dinner, while my wife and I were talking to Bill about how the book was going.

"What are you going to call it?" he asked in that casual way of his.

"Think," I said. "I've worked for you for the best part of six years now. There's only one title I could possibly use, isn't there?"

"Smoke and mirrors?" ventured Cunningham, with a sad little grin.

"Smoke and mirrors," I said.

I am grateful not only to Cunningham and Global, who allowed me time to write the book, but to my wife, who read the manuscript as it came out of the typewriter and who managed to tone down both outrageous spelling and outrageous propositions. At her behest, I apologize for using "he" in places where "she" would have been equally appropriate.

If I have managed to convey something of the complexity, the excitement, and the opportunity that exists in television news to the long-suffering viewer, or if I have managed to talk one young man or woman of quality into a career in television journalism, the effort will have been worth it. I hope too that it makes some key people angry, in the CBC, the CRTC, in Parliament, and in the nation's newsrooms. Perhaps they'll be moved to do something about the declining state of television while it still has some intelligent viewers.

PT
Warkworth, Ontario,
September 1, 1979

CHAPTER ONE

The Fifth Floor

Television news, as far as I am concerned, is like strong drink. When the madness is on me, I can't imagine doing anything else, or even that there is anything else worth doing. Sometimes, when I am shooting film in a strange new location with a good camera crew, I chortle inwardly. At times like those it is hard to believe that people actually pay me for what I do. At other times, after unbroken weeks and months at the anchor desk, with the jungle growing in on me again, I have saner moments, moments when I wish I'd stuck to my first love, archaeology, or that my branch of the Trueman family had never left the soil. And I remember that my television career began badly, as a waking nightmare.

Many of the people who are prominent in the Canadian industry today shared that nightmare, for they too had their start at the CBC, on the fifth floor of the old Jarvis Street television building in Toronto. Much of what is wrong with television news in this country is due to the fact that so many of us have our roots in the same place. Much of what is right about it is due to that fact too. For even those who have never worked on the fifth floor, where the national newscasts are produced, owe the place their standards. The good grey CBC News was first, more than a quarter-century ago, and for the serious viewer it remains first in a lacklustre field.

The fifth floor is the home base for the CBC's national news service. In the afternoon, it gathers and feeds national and international items to the CBC's regional newsrooms for their early newscasts; and at night, it lines up, writes, and produces the major news vehicle of the Canadian day, the CBC TV News at 11:00 P.M., "The National." The CBC's is by far the largest Canadian TV news operation, in terms of budget, manpower, and output. And it is still the largest in terms of ratings, despite the initial promise of the Lloyd and Harvey show, and the fact that the CBC keeps changing faces.

In the three-year span from early 1974 to late 1976, when CTV finally filched Lloyd Robertson from the CBC, "The National" increased its lead over CTV's late newscast by some 200,000 viewers. According to the Bureau of Broadcast Measurement (BBM), the CBC's 11:00 newscast was pulling 1,414,000 viewers by late 1976. CTV's rating was 997,000 viewers. CTV points out that because of the CBC's big reach, it has a potential audience of 6,889,000 households, 6 per cent larger than the CTV potential of 6,501,000 households. And the CTV flacks never fail to note that their newscast consistently outdraws "The National" in several of the major urban centres, including the grand prize of the Canadian marketplace, Toronto. The implication is that the people in the boondocks don't know any better.

But CTV's huffing and puffing can't conceal the fact that the theft of Robertson hasn't really worked. The Lloyd and Harvey combination closed the gap for a time, and by November of 1978 they were breathing down "The National's" neck, just 150,000 viewers behind a worried CBC. At the end of Knowlton Nash's first week, that same month, BBM awarded the race to CTV, with 1,346,000 adult viewers as opposed to the CBC's 1,323,000.

If CTV relaxed at that point, it relaxed too soon. At the end of the four-week winter rating period, which ended February 11, 1979, CTV had skidded badly. "The National's" average in that period had picked up nicely, to 1,458,000 adult viewers. CTV averaged only 1,182,000 viewers in that same important period. In the 1979 spring ratings, "The National" settled a little, to 1,355,000 viewers, still slightly better than it had been when Nash took over. But, at one point, CTV had actually dipped below the magic million (to 905,000 viewers in the week of April 9 - 15), and it levelled out at what must have been a disappointing 1,190,000 viewer average for the spring period. "The National" had a

400,000 bulge in the week of June 11-17, but in the doldrums of July 23-29, it shrunk to 100,000 viewers.

In the early fall rating period of 1979, September 24 to October 28, the CBC averaged 1,242,400 adult viewers, as opposed to CTV's 1,094,600, a slow beginning for a new season. In Toronto, which is supposed to be the key to it all, ''The National'' was averaging only 6 per cent of the adult audience against CTV's 8 per cent, proof positive, if anyone still needed it, that both major newscasts are aired too late.

And so, somewhat uneasily, ''The National'' continued to hold the lead. And once again, the CBC's pollsters must have felt vindicated. They have always argued that given an adequate minimum performance, it doesn't matter who reads the news. It is the institution that counts, not the face of the latest reader.

But there isn't much doubt that the man who reads the news makes a difference, whether or not it shows up in the ratings. The audience relations people at the CBC have what they call an ''enjoyment index,'' but a poll doesn't exist for credibility.

In the beginning, the CBC decided to remain with a tradition derived from radio, and before that the BBC, namely that the man who fronted the news was simply a reader, a staff announcer. And over the years, successive layers of CBC management signed away their rights to change their minds. Negotiators for the corporation not only agreed that no one but an announcer could read the news, but also agreed that no one but a news writer, a member of the American Newspaper Guild (in the CBC's Canadian Wire Service Guild bargaining unit), could write it. What this meant, in the words of Bill Cunningham, now Global's vice-president for News, was that the CBC's anchorman could never be anything more than a ''news actor.'' Even now, the hosts of the CBC's national news can only read what is handed to them or face a Guild grievance.

This wanton frittering away of the CBC's rights has caused trouble from the beginning. One of the earliest national news hosts, Larry Henderson, left because he had ambitions as a correspondent which couldn't be fulfilled as long as he was the resident announcer on the CBC's major newscast. Earl Cameron, perhaps the best newsreader who ever graced ''The National,'' was forced out because Cunningham, then the executive producer, wanted to pressure the corporation into an accommodation that would allow the newscast to be anchored by a bona fide newsman, who would write and read his own material. But the corporation wouldn't push hard enough, and Stanley Burke was a casualty of that timidity.

The situation was further aggravated by the fact that the CBC tried to cover its tracks at the bargaining table. As a result of the pressure to give the newsreader American-style "anchorman" status, the CBC began to fudge the issue publicly, and even internally. The corporation's public relations people tried to cast "The National's" newsreader as a real newsman, and, on at least one occasion, news executives managed to lure a staff announcer into the job with vague promises of meaningful participation.

In the beginning, the chief Canadian resources that went into television news were the film cameramen and film editors who had been responsible for Canadian newsreels, and reporters and deskmen from radio news. But very early on, because the British had had a head start in television news, the CBC began importing expertise from the United Kingdom. At the time, because the fledgling service could not hope to cover the world on its own, it began procuring foreign news film from the major networks in the United States. The impact on Canadian TV news was, and is, enormous. Even today, a disproportionate number of news professionals in this country came originally from the U.K., and all three networks continue to depend heavily on the American news services for overseas footage.

But this wasn't all the CBC borrowed. And in the view of some television veterans, it wound up with the worst features of the BBC plus the weaknesses of the U.S. networks. The CBC eschewed the service system of broadcasting, as practised by the BBC, and embraced the commercial, populist philosophy of the U.S. networks. It rejected the lean administrative structure of a CBS, and instead adopted the bureaucratic chaos of the BBC.

And the imported influences, of British personnel and American film, have helped shape television news and Canadian perceptions generally, in a way that may never be quantified. The British, by and large, have helped us to nurture our own neurotic suspicion that Canada and Canadians are second rate. British television is probably the best in the English-speaking world, so the professional standards its escapees brought with them were very high. But it would be difficult to estimate what that simple fact has done to Canadian self-esteem, and how much Canadian television's perception of uniquely Canadian problems has been dulled by non-Canadian eyes in key places at the wrong times. American film, appearing night after night on our screens, has at the same time helped to give us a distinctly American view of the outside world.

This was never more dangerous than during the Vietnam war, when the CBC, tempted by dramatic American battle footage, found itself parroting the line taken by most American correspondents about the morality and progress of the war. The CBC, it is true, wiped the American sound tracks of everything but artillery, mortar, and machine-gun fire, and wrote its own scripts for the announcer to read voiceover. But a good film script is dictated by the pictures, and the available information was usually limited to what was on the sound track originally. So even after the insertion of the Canadian filter, the message was American, its outlines dictated too often by the Pentagon. The situation was not helped by the fact that throughout the war, the CBC did not identify such films as procured material. It wasn't until Global News went on the air in 1974, that the larger networks were shamed into the identification of film which was not their own. And such identification still isn't automatic, by either the CBC or CTV networks, or their individual stations.

I had been in newspapers for the best part of fifteen years when I first joined the CBC, as a news writer, in the summer of 1968. I wasn't prepared for the human zoo that was waiting to absorb me on the fifth floor. I had stumbled into journalism during my junior year in straight arts at the University of New Brunswick. The college paper, *The Brunswickan*, needed a sports editor, and in desperation, I was offered the job. Printer's ink soon obscured any tendency I might have had towards scholarship, and I went to work full time for the *Ottawa Journal* in the spring of 1955, after a disastrous and incomplete senior year at Carleton. I worked the "night police beat" at the *Journal*, transferred briefly to public relations at the CNR and rejoined the human race a few months later

17

as a general reporter at the *Montreal Star*. I was married in 1956, and by late 1957, found myself in New York, for the *Star*, writing a highly personal general interest column, which appeared four times a week. In late 1959, I was transferred to the United Nations, to write an international affairs column for Canada-Wide features and to cover the United Nations for the *Star*. In 1962, I was transferred to Washington, where I stayed until shortly after Lyndon Johnson's election, late in 1964. I worked for a time for the *Toronto Star*, in its Ottawa bureau, and then quit to become the national director of the United Nations Association in Canada.

By the time I arrived at the CBC, I'd run up some pretty respectable mileage, but most of it was in print, and far removed from my home base. What I knew about radio and television was largely as a listener and a viewer. I had done the occasional commentary for CBC radio, some news reports for CBC's early-morning radio, and the occasional television "Viewpoint" for the slot following the national news. I had known Knowlton Nash and James M. ("Don" to his friends) Minifie in Washington. I had known Stanley Burke in New York, and the executives in the CBC office there, John Dunn and Dorothy McCullum. I met and got to know Tom Gould, when he succeeded Burke in New York, and through all of them, met Don MacDonald, one of the founders of CBC TV News, one of the nicest, most normal people in the business. I had even met Bill Cunningham, while he was a producer with CBC "Newsmagazine." But knowing them hadn't prepared me for the fifth floor either.

Some years earlier, I had applied for the CBC's prestigious London job, when the correspondent's position fell vacant, and I had had a wryly amused rejection from Bill Hogg, then the chief news editor. But I didn't seriously go after a CBC job until 1968, when I became ill and was forced to resign from the United Nations Association. Naturally I was still interested in a reporter's job, partly because the bulk of my experience had been as a reporter, and partly because I fancied myself in a trenchcoat. I had dickered with CTV for a time, but Charles Templeton, who then headed CTV News, and who had seemed quite keen in the beginning, took a hard look at the screen test and his nerve failed him. And so, when the CTV negotiations trailed off into an awkward silence, I resumed talking to the CBC. Through the intervention of Knowlton Nash, who was then wheeling and dealing in network politics from his base as a Washington correspondent, I talked to Don MacDonald, the TV news chief, and to Joe Schlesinger, the executive producer of "The National." Finally, it was agreed that I would come on strength as an "editor 'C'," that is, as a writer on the national news desk.

I agreed to accept an inside job for several reasons. In the first place, it seemed to be the only way to get a foot in the door. In the second place, there was my health, and for a while at least I could see that it might make some sense to avoid the rigours of the road. And in the third place, the CBC offered me a fairly standard under-the-counter supplemental payment, which, with overtime, would allow me to live above the union scale. The fact that it was under-the-counter, and the fact that the CBC had to offer it at all, should have served as a warning. Union-management relations were foul and getting fouler, and I was to spend the next four years, one way or another, right in the middle. From the beginning, my fellow guildsmen suspected that I had been offered not only a financial deal, but some kind of career deal as well. In fact, I hadn't been offered anything in terms of a better job, beyond the suggestion that if things worked out, I might move eventually into reporting. But when I was made the executive producer, quite unexpectedly a few months later, it was, at least for the more militant unionists, a suspicion confirmed.

When I arrived on the fifth floor, there was only one familiar face in the newsroom. It was that of my old friend Stanley Burke, late of New York, Paris, and London, the current reader of the national news. And Stanley's face wasn't in evidence for more than a couple of hours a day.

The newsroom, like Stanley, was a legacy of Bill Cunningham's brief but vigorous reign as executive producer. There were two long desks and an array of monitors at the north end of the room where the national newscasts were lined up and written. In the middle of the floor was the Toronto regional operation, where a roster of freelance cameramen and soundmen hung out, waiting for the day's assignments. At the south end of the floor was a film library and a couple of rooms for "Newsmagazine." The film editors' cubicles ran along the west wall, where there was additional space for the wire machines and graphic artists. The east wall, whose windows had an uninspiring view of the girders that supported the Jarvis Street television transmission mast, was executive row. The northeast corner was the sanctum of the chief news editor, or head of News, as he was later known, then occupied by Ray Hazzan, known as "the Asp." Joe Schlesinger, the executive producer, had a narrow cubicle on the west wall. Its most memorable feature was a green, vinyl-covered couch, which a previous producer was supposed to have purchased for the selection and training of script assistants. Stanley Burke had no office at all, just a desk and a phone. Burke's basket overflowed with letters from female viewers who lusted for him in the privacy of their living rooms. Not that Stanley showed them around; he was too much of a gentleman for that. It's just that when he didn't answer their letters they called the newsroom in person, breathing heavily. We all had to deal with them.

The average viewer may be surprised to learn that the people who produce this country's television news, myself included, are part of a subculture that bears no relationship whatever to the image presented by a Stanley Burke or a Knowlton Nash. They are neither wholesome, the way Stanley looked, nor good and grey the way Knowlton looks. As a matter of fact, Stanley himself is a lot of things, and wholesome is only one of them. And Knowlton is, well, Knowlton. The people in television news do not wear snap-brim fedoras or wear press cards in their hat bands, but in a way they are much closer to the old "Front Page" image than the average newspaperman. As newspapers have come of age, they have attracted more serious, disciplined people, many of them specialists. In the old days, newspapermen were hard drinking, colourful, and proud of the fact that they were generalists, that they could do any job on any paper, anytime, anywhere. The profile of an old-time newspaperman, if you subtract the fedora and a bottle and add a jean jacket and a joint, is almost a profile for the average man or woman in the off-camera jobs in a television newsroom. One image, of course, is just about as overdrawn as the other. But in the cliché, there is more than a grain of truth.

On the fifth floor, the film shipping desk was near the elevator. It was staffed, most days, by a dwarf known as "Snarly," who had the deep, booming voice of a 260-pound tackle. He terrified telephone operators and airline express clerks from Hong Kong to Moscow. There was a reporter who was fired for "creating" a piece of wire copy about the supposed arrest of a CBC soundman in the Middle East, and leaving it for an unsuspecting late editor, who put it on the last regional newscast of the day, after the late movie. The incident might have been forgotten had the soundman's family not been informed, and if the corporation had not in good faith involved External Affairs. There was a fiery union leader, best remembered for the line he delivered in negotiations when he found himself across the table from some management representative whom he considered too junior for the job at hand.

"Why should I deal with the monkey when I can talk to the organ grinder?" he asked.

They got him the organ grinder.

There was a producer who set fires in waste-baskets. There was a writer who tore fire extinguishers off the wall to deal with the flaming waste-baskets, and who once punched holes in the wall with karate chops. There was a writer known as "The Trembling Airsucker" because of a curious habit he had when a newscast was in jeopardy. He pursed his lips and inhaled audibly. There was a well-endowed female director, who, after the well-known instant coffee commercial of the time, was known as "The Star with the Jars on Top." There was a former English sportswriter who wrote plays, and drank scotch and ginger beer. There was another writer who could hardly bear to come to work at all, and whose increasingly lengthy absences made us all rich on overtime until, like the Cheshire cat's smile, he finally vanished entirely. I don't think he quit. He just stopped coming. There was a reporter known as "The Flasher" because he had once been falsely portrayed in an elaborate practical joke as an ex-priest, who had been defrocked for whipping open his raincoat. The joke was soon forgotten, but the handle lingered on. There was a line-up editor who pulled at his hair when he was under pressure. By the end of the shift, since he was always under pressure, it stood straight up from his head, in spiky tufts.

There was a cameraman known as ''Lunch Hooks'' because of his fondness for food, on and off the job, and his girth was the butt of many a cruel office joke. There was the time when he spotted a lunch counter on the other side of an expressway, and split his pants crawling over the median barrier for a bowl of soup. And then, of course, there was me, a pedestrian addition, by and large, but not without moments of conspicuous achievement. Such as the time I got blind drunk on my day off, found my way somehow to the fifth floor, offered to be ill all over a regional news supervisor I hadn't exchanged eight words with, and threatened to punch a film editor I scarcely knew. There was something about the atmosphere of the place that did things to you.

The fifth floor was alive with rackets. One of the most interesting was one that gave a reporter or a writer his day off and overtime too. The newsroom pay scales in 1968 ranged from about $10,000 to $12,000 a year, but it was not uncommon for those at the lower end of the scale to pick up another $4,500 in overtime, and from time to time, a $12,000 job was parleyed into $19,000 or even $20,000 a year. The most popular racket was worked by people in pairs. One of them would book off sick on his illicit partner's scheduled day off, and suggest that the partner might be available for some overtime. The harassed duty producer, anxious to bring the shift up to strength as quickly as possible, would take the line of least resistance, and call the man known to be available. Then the procedure would be reversed. The man who filled in would book off sick when he was supposed to be working, on his now-recovered partner's day off, suggest that the partner would be willing to work, and one more circuit of this unholy but profitable alliance would be complete. Others used CBC film and equipment for money-making ventures on the side. The correspondents' expense accounts were notorious. One of the most colourful offenders filed a sizable claim for ''piranha repellent'' and was reimbursed for it.

This den of iniquity would have been an amusing place to work if it hadn't been for the fact that relations between the Guild (the writers and reporters union) and CBC management were abysmal. Suspicion and resentment permeated that stale space like mustard gas. You could almost taste it. It erupted visibly from time to time in nasty little anonymous notes that appeared on the main notice board.

But the salt in the union's wounds was Stanley Burke. When I got there, Stanley was an anachronism. He'd been lured out of an interesting correspondent's job by what was then a big dollar (I think about $30,000 a year) and Bill Cunningham's intention to make an honest anchorman out of the newsreader. Stanley was erudite, handsome, and an experienced reporter and analyst. But he was hopelessly underemployed as a mere newsreader, and unable because of the impasse between the unions to do anything but to accept delivery of a script and read it. The Guild disliked him so intensely that they watched him like a hawk. If he tried to dot an "i" on his own, without clearing it with a line-up editor or a producer, there was a grievance. At the end, Stanley came in a few minutes ahead of the Maritime feed at 10:00 P.M. Toronto time, put on his pancake, read through the script, and took it to air. Partly because he was bored and hence careless, he made mistakes. Instead of commiserating, some of the guildsmen were gleeful about it. They called him "Stanley Stumbles," and when he hit a bad patch in the script and had trouble on the air, they saw it as a victory. Stanley wouldn't have had that kind of trouble if he had been able to write his own scripts. He wasn't a trained announcer, although he became very good at announcing. He was a reporter and a correspondent, and he was denied the right to exercise his craft.

Occasionally, Burke lost his temper. I'll never forget the sixth of June in the late sixties, when we sent Norman DePoe to Normandy to do an anniversary piece on the Allied landing. It was vintage DePoe. That hoarse, whisky-soaked voice was, for that night, the voice of the Canadian Legion. His report was sensitive and moving. And it was the final visual item in the newscast that night. For some reason or other, probably because he needed to make up the time, the line-up editor insisted that despite his protests, Stanley read a closing on-camera item after the film, and before the sign-off. It was probably something light and amusing, a typical closer. But on that particular night, after DePoe's haunting piece from Normandy, it was tasteless and out of place. Burke read the item, signed off stonily, and stormed up into the control room. Swearing horribly, he flung his script in the general direction of the line-up editor and strode from the room.

That incident took place because Stanley had been forced to function as a news actor, with no choice but to read his lines on cue. The man on the air, because it is his face, his voice, and his personality that are chiefly identified with the newscast, has a proprietary feeling for it that a line-up editor, preoccupied with timing and pacing, sometimes doesn't have. A good anchorman, who senses the impact of his material, would no more tell a funny story after a film on our glorious dead than he would crack a joke in tragic circumstances if he were a guest in someone's living room. In my view, it is very nearly criminal to deprive a news host of the right to exercise normal human judgement and sensitivity.

The pressure is so constant in television news that it is often difficult for line-up editors and producers to stand back and take a long view. A man with his finger in the dyke is the last one you'd ask for the overall flood position. And yet, in Canadian television, it is the men with their fingers in the dyke who determine what makes the newscast. In the daily grind of filling sixteen minutes, or twenty-five minutes, or forty-eight minutes, you tend not to think about the cumulative effect of a week's news, or a month's news, or a year's news, so the disciplines are daily, and if you err, it tends to be on the side of caution and responsibility.

Television, Robert MacNeil suggested in *The People Machine,* acts as a cheering section for the side that has already won. David Halberstam, in *The Powers That Be,* noted that there is an unwritten law of American journalism, which holds that the more powerful the medium, the more carefully it must conform to society's and government's norms. It is held dangerous to be too right too quickly.

"Part of this," Halberstam wrote, "is born out of a need for respectability, and a desire for legitimacy and a fear of disturbing the status quo, and part of it is born out of a very healthy sense that if the platform is that powerful, personal opinions are almost dangerous, that no one journalist should be that powerful.... Thus almost from the start of television there was an unconscious decision at the networks to limit the autonomy of the network news show.''

When you consider that the BBC and the American networks between them have been the unconscious models for CBC television news, it is no wonder that ''The National'' sometimes appears aenemic. Caution is always the refuge of the uncertain. It is safer to be a little daring in one's dress or grooming than in the realm of ideas. The commercial pressures of American network television, which ensure the continuing triumph of the bland, are not present for the CBC. But in a sense the real and imagined political pressures that haunt the corporation are even more insidious than those of the dollar. It is much safer for CBC News to maintain the status quo, to pretend that political balance consists of three twenty-second voice clips from each of the major parties. And if the politicians aren't enough to inhibit them, there is always the licence and the Canadian Radio Television Commission.

That is one reason that the CBC has had to live with a haemorrhage of good people. Don Cameron, the vice-president of News at CTV, was once a CBC producer. Tom Gould, Cameron's predecessor at CTV, was a CBC correspondent. Bill Cunningham, the vice-president of News at Global, is a former CBC producer and correspondent, and like most of the people who have had to leave the CBC, is bitter about the fact that we're not all together in one place trying to put out the kind of newscast that the country deserves. There is a case to be made for the assertion that if all the people who had their start in television news at the CBC were back at the old stand with a bold leader and a reasonable mandate that the country would have such a newscast.

I have often wondered what sort of direction CBC News might have taken if, after the Second World War, someone like Matthew Halton, who was to Canada what Ed Murrow was to the United States, had returned to Toronto to head CBC News. There is no doubt about the effect that Murrow had on CBS, and continued to have long after he'd left. Excellence tends to hire excellence. And once established, excellence is not easily erased, despite the commercial and political qualms of senior management. Murrow left CBS in 1961, but David Halberstam is convinced that it was Murrow's influence, ultimately, that made the network's coverage superior years later during the Vietnam war.

"While the CBS report from Saigon had its faults – the lack of time, the lack of a cumulative meaningful texture, an emphasis on bang-bang in film – it nonetheless distinguished itself by its coverage of Vietnam," Halberstam wrote. "To the American military, it was known as the Communist Broadcasting Station. But CBS was better than the other two networks, and by journalistic consensus, the two best television reporters of the war were [Morley] Safer and his younger colleague Jack Laurence. It was the CBS tradition that made the network special, the tradition that began with Murrow and still lived and meant that CBS attracted better people and had higher professional standards."

If Matthew Halton had been at the helm of CBC News, hiring his people, implanting his values, putting his imprint on CBC News, nurturing the kind of sensitive reporting that distinguished his own war-time file from Europe, would we have lost a Morley Safer to the Murrow flame? Would Peter Jennings be working for ABC in London? Would Robert MacNeil be hosting PBS's nightly "MacNeil-Lehrer Report"? And would many of the good Canadians who stayed in Canada be outside the CBC, trying to do the CBC's job with inadequate budgets and news machines? I don't think so.

But there was no Halton in charge of CBC News. After the war, radio news remained in the hands of the disseminators. The gatherers were few and far between, and they stayed outside, with the glamour, in the cold. The men in charge of radio news were good men, many of them, but they were deskmen rather than reporters, fixers rather than doers. They understood the urgency of news, but not its drama. The fires that should have burned in their bellies were instead a guttering, CBC-issue flame, a flame that was snuffed out time and time again in an avalanche of bureaucratic paper.

In the early days of television, the problem was compounded because of the mysteries of the new medium. Journalists who knew anything about film and television were scarce. And so television fell into the hands of the radio men, who in turn were pre-empted by a rising cadre of television directors, people who knew how to direct a television program from a control room, but who knew nothing whatever about news or journalistic principles. The directors held sway in CBC TV News until the early sixties.

In the meantime, the new young breed of television news journalists, who were not trusted by the CBC hierarchy, fulminated in vain as news values were subordinated to program values. They had a reasonably free hand in the gathering process, but when it came to putting news on the air they were overruled. And the two could not be divorced. The example that stands out in one veteran's mind was being forced to do a news interview in a set with arches and Roman columns because a fey but powerful director felt it was "right."

This is not to say that CBC News didn't have moments of excellence. It did, and does increasingly rarely. I remember some of those early stand-up reports from Parliament Hill by people like Blair Fraser. That was in the days before the Press Gallery would admit broadcast journalists. Fraser, as the Ottawa editor of *Maclean's* magazine, was already accredited, and he did reports for the CBC on a freelance basis. James M. Minifie, the CBC's long-time Washington correspondent, was more comfortable with radio than he ever was with television, but despite the unsympathetic medium, his intellect and his passion bled through. Norman DePoe did some of the best reporting we've ever had from Parliament Hill. Michael Maclear beat the world time and time again with his reports from Southeast Asia. But all of those people, except for Fraser, who wasn't on staff, and who therefore didn't have to survive on that hind tit of mediocrity, were demoralized in the end by the vacuum through which they had to file.

And the fifth floor wasn't always merely a vacuum. The people who worked there had their favourites, and the correspondents were rarely among them. Instead of working to air their material to advantage, for the sake of the newscast and the CBC, they took great delight in isolating the failures of those in the field, and gleefully worked against them. There was little *esprit de corps* on the fifth floor when I got there.

The result was that CBC News management was often preoccupied with fighting brushfire wars among their staff members and between News and other departments. A sneaky underground tussle was in progress between News and Current Affairs, a legacy of the "Seven Days" insurrection. The News people had not only disapproved of the "Seven Days" brand of journalism, but of its methods. "Seven Days" had a reputation for stealing news film, butchering original footage, and jamming it on the air without any regard for its archival importance. And so News worked actively against Current Affairs, despite the fact that both departments had been lumped together, for the first time, under Knowlton Nash, newly appointed as the head of TV Information Programming. There was almost as big a rift between TV news and radio news. Some correspondents and reporters were designated as double-duty. That is, while they were doing a piece for television, they were also expected to work up a piece for radio. But even when they obeyed the rules, there was trouble. TV News was always complaining because the radio version of the feature story was available and being used a day or two before the television item could possibly be shipped, cut, and aired. Under Nash, some attempts were made to reconcile these counter-productive differences, but the CBC's internal structure tended to defeat such efforts, and Information Programming's various factions were generally engaged in throat-cutting competition. The nightmare was pretty vivid.

CHAPTER TWO

"Rotten Management"

I had been working at the CBC only a few months as a writer on the national news when I was appointed executive producer. My news background was fairly solid, at least in newspapers, but I was in no way prepared, professionally or mentally, for taking the helm of the country's most prestigious newscast. I think I knew it, because I fortified myself so thoroughly the first day on the job that the new head of News, Joe Schlesinger, who had just vacated the executive producer's office, had to pour me into his car and take me home.

I had been there just long enough to know what I was up against — the staff on one hand and senior news management on the other. Several months before, one of the news producers had admitted to me that he and several militant members of the Guild had met secretly with Judy LaMarsh, then the Secretary of State, to fill her in on what was wrong with the CBC. That meeting, and I suspect others, led her to that famous outburst on the floor of the Commons about the corporation's "rotten management." She never spoke truer words. The CBC was solid jello, right to the top, and I quickly became part of the corporate dessert.

Schlesinger was my immediate boss, a Czechoslovakian Jew who had emigrated to British Columbia as a young man, where he went to the University of British Columbia and ultimately acquired membership in the so-called "B.C. mafia," a force to be reckoned with in Canadian journalism. Schlesinger was a good newsman with a solid print background. He had been, at one stage in his career, the assistant managing editor of the Paris edition of the *New*

York Herald Tribune, and I think had worked for the *Toronto Star* for a time before being shuttled in the back door of CBC News in the time-honoured tradition. Joe's worst quality as an administrator was his ill-concealed contempt for most of the people in the newsroom. His sardonic smile, his impatience, and his guttural utterances, in a heavy Eastern European accent, did not endear him to the other inhabitants of the fifth-floor zoo.

He did better in the other relationship, with management. He was smart and tough and honest, and although he too at times succumbed to corporate gamesmanship, he was, while he lasted, a voice of reason in what was then the network's administration building, "The Kremlin," across the parking lot. Like me, at that time, however, he didn't know enough about television news, and perhaps it was that knowledge that made us both restless.

At least twice before my term was over as executive producer, I tried to get out. The first time I called Keith Murrow, the director of the Newfoundland region, to see if he had anything I could do there. I had long had a love affair with that province, in some ways Canada's last southern frontier, and there were moments during my life in the executive producer's cell when I would have considered sweeping floors in Newfoundland in exchange for freedom. As it happened, when I wanted out, there was nothing doing.

About the time we moved Bill Cunningham from Hong Kong to London, I was ready to quit again. I still had visions of myself in a trenchcoat and so I asked Nash to consider me for the Hong Kong bureau. For a while, the prospects looked good. But I was ill-advised enough to leave Toronto for a vacation on Prince Edward Island, before it was resolved, and when a series of frantic messages finally reached me, and I rang Nash from a public telephone booth on Stanhope Beach, I learned that Schlesinger's need was greater than mine. He had just resigned, Nash informed me, as head of News, and he too wanted Hong Kong. Would I step aside, and let Schlesinger's name stand? I agreed, and in retrospect, it was probably a good thing that I did. For one thing, Schlesinger quickly became one of the best correspondents in CBC history. For another thing, at that point in my career, I might have botched the job.

One of the first things that Nash had managed to do when he took over as head of TV Information Programming was to institute a nightly film feed from the regions to Toronto, so that the early newscasts and "The National" could for the first time carry same-day news from right across the country. Until that time, except on special occasions, film from the outlying parts of Canada had been air-shipped to Toronto, which meant that much of the time it didn't make "The National" until the following day. Nash insisted on calling the nightly internal feed "an electronic highway," a phrase he used to some effect to dramatize what we were doing in an endless series of speeches to service clubs and other worthy institutions. It was a good move, establishing that nightly feed, but most of us, Nash included, didn't envisage the problems that the new facility would create. What it meant for a long time was that we put regional items on the air which weren't broad enough for a national newscast, either because they had been shot and scripted with the regional newscast in mind, or because the reporters we used didn't have savvy enough to put a regional story into a meaningful national context.

When Nash's highway was inaugurated, Schlesinger insisted that we flaunt its existence somehow on "The National." As I recall it, Ross McLean, who was then once again undergoing a period of corporate underemployment, sat down with us. Between us, we devised a series of graphics and labels to underline the fact of the new feed. The details, mercifully, have escaped me. But I do remember that on "The National," for a time, we identified late visual items with a graphic that read "Nightline" and backed it up by using the same word in the introductory script, the intro.

It was one time when I was grateful that a newscast is like a vegetable garden. If the executive producer doesn't weed it every day, the rows, that is the established order, quickly become obscured. I stopped weeding, and "Nightline" and all its tacky relations slowly disappeared. The news staff, quite rightly, wiser in the ways of television than either Schlesinger or me, had viewed it from the first as an abomination. The best newscast, I soon learned, is a clean one.

And I also learned that it was easier to alter the course and speed of the *Queen Mary* than to fiddle with the flagship of CBC News. I had long felt that television news had some sort of responsibility to cover business, not simply to make Bay Street happy, but to give the average citizen the kind of basic information he needed to make reasonably intelligent investments and purchases. And so, when a young woman with the right qualifications walked in my door from Winnipeg, I decided to try a nightly business report on "The National." It wasn't a particularly auspicious beginning. It was almost totally a stock market report, for one thing. But it deserved a better chance than it got – a single week, five nightly reports. I hadn't cleared it sufficiently up the line, with senior management, and I hadn't cleared it down the line, with the Guild.

I learned early on that playing dumb was sometimes the only way to survive the awful squeeze between senior management and the newsroom. But playing dumb was no substitute for authority. And I soon learned where the real authority lay when senior management decided they'd had enough of Stanley Burke.

Stanley had openly declared for the Biafran side in the brutal Nigerian civil war. Not on the air, of course, because he was a gelded anchorman, but in speaking engagements. Nash decided that Stanley's Biafran convictions were an embarrassment to the news service, and so he called the two of us in, and put it squarely to the offending reader. Stanley would have to choose between Biafra and the national news. Stanley chose Biafra.

Nash's argument was that being associated with the Biafran cause damaged Burke's credibility as the host of "The National." That credibility, of course, was based on the specious public assumption that Burke had some influence over what went into his newscast, an assumption that CBC management didn't want to disturb. That piece of hypocrisy cost me one of the best front men we ever had on the newscast. Even with both hands tied, Stanley had managed to invest "The National" with grace and excellence.

As it turned out, I couldn't, as executive producer, do anything more about Burke's replacement than I'd been able to do about his leaving. A panel was convened, applications were called for, and we began to hold auditions. At one stage, ever the optimist, I applied myself, and was duly given a script to read. I was sweaty and nervous, and when I came back to the control room from the studio, I knew immediately from Schlesinger's wry amusement that I was going to remain the executive producer.

So at that stage, I began pushing hard for my own first nominee, Peter Reilly. The biggest handicap in the selling of Reilly was his reliability. No one doubted his talent, but there was grave doubt that he would be able to deliver the goods, night after night, for any protracted period. As executive producer, I was prepared to live with that, and said so. He would have been great for "The National." That craggy Irish face and his tough, urgent delivery would have taken some of the good grey edge off the news without damaging our authority. Reilly would have been the perfect foil for CTV's Harvey Kirck.

But it wasn't to be. Nash and company decided it was going to be Warren Davis, a CBC staff announcer who seemed to be the only man in the "announce" office who didn't really want the job. Like many of the corporation's golden throats, Davis was no dummy. And in program areas outside of news, which were not affected by the absurd union restrictions that applied to the fifth floor, he was allowed to think, write his own scripts, ad lib when it seemed appropriate, and otherwise participate actively in the program he was taking to air. Davis wanted no part of the mechanical prison that was reading the national news.

And so Nash set out to convince him. I listened in growing horror as he dangled one carrot after another. Nash was difficult to pin down – and Lord knows Davis tried – but the Information boss managed to give the impression that the situation on the fifth floor was much more elastic than it really was. Yes, it might be difficult for Davis to sit down at a typewriter and actually write his own script, but there were ways that Davis could make his presence felt. (The only time Davis managed to make a personal comment on the air was one night in the intro to a southern Ontario storm story. It contained a personal reference to the beating his own fruit trees had taken, and I wrote that for him.) As this strange conversation with Nash continued, Davis made the point that he was very good at editing video tape. Would he be allowed to edit tape now and then? The implication was that he would. One way or another, Nash managed to convey his conviction that in a consultative capacity, Davis would have considerable input not only on assignments, but on the line-up, the way the news was put together. It was probably cowardly of me to remain silent, but I managed to convince myself that Nash must have known something I didn't about the relations between the two unions that made the job he was describing a little more than a fond hope. To my disquiet, Davis bought it, and took on ''The National.'' Less than a year later, when it had long been obvious that his situation was no different than that of the readers who preceded him, he quit, justifiably bitter. I had no hand in the appointment of Davis, and no hand either in the appointment of Lloyd Robertson, his successor. As a matter of fact, I opposed Robertson's appointment.

The only battle I won over Robertson was with the corporation's public relations department. I got a call one morning from a young information officer, who was clearly only checking with me because CBC courtesies demanded it. He wanted to do a series of magazine advertisements, which would have identified Robertson with the gathering and preparation of the newscast. He wanted to illustrate at least one of the ads with a picture of Robertson, typewriter in hand, ascending the steps of an airplane.

I said no to the ads, as flatly as I could. Incredulous, the young man remonstrated with me. I was firm. I explained that the ads would be a lie. The implication of the photograph would be that Robertson actually gathered and wrote news. The young man assured me that the accompanying copy would not make that claim. There would only be the impression left by the picture. I told him that the answer was still No and that in this instance at least, my No was a veto.

Then the screaming started. Who the hell did I think I was? He would, he suggested, have my ass. But I never heard from him again, and that kind of ad never appeared, at least during the time I was associated with the CBC News.

It seems incredible in retrospect, but in the fall of 1970, Canada's flagship newscast was still not entirely in colour. Officially, as a matter of fact, it was still completely black and white. The only reason that Burke and the studio portion of the newscast was in colour was that Schlesinger, operating like Lord Beaverbrook as the minister responsible for British aircraft production during the war, had simply hijacked two colour cameras from Parliament Hill. Of course the visual material we were getting from the American networks was in colour, but the bulk of our own film was still black and white, which gave the newscast a piebald effect that was unsettling, at least to anyone with a colour set. I could never quite understand the corporation's colour blindness, but the story was told that the negative outlook began with George Davidson, the president. It was said that Davidson's own television set was black and white, and that it was so old it had a round screen. True or not, this explanation was widely believed, and there seems to be little doubt that the decision to keep "The National" in black and white had to do with senior management's desire to convince the Treasury Board that we weren't frittering away the taxpayers' money.

When I first became executive producer, I decided it was time to enter the twentieth century. So we began shooting colour on a day-to-day basis. On some days, we called it colour trials. We said we were putting colour through the system so that film cameramen would become familiar with its use and so that we could see which of the various film labs we used across the country could process colour. Montreal, I remember, couldn't handle it, and neither could some of the labs in the West and the Maritimes. On other days, we shot colour, we said because the film we were shooting was of archival value, and it was important that it be in colour for use in what was bound to be a coloured future. Neither argument was particularly telling, but they were sufficient. And finally, on October 26, 1970, the colour ban was lifted.

"Up until now," I noted in a memo to the staff, "the colour we have been shooting has been done in the face of an edict forbidding it, quite apart from budgetary considerations.

"Now we are being allowed to shoot colour, but to put it in its simplest terms, we'll have to do it on a black and white budget. If we can't do it on a black and white budget, the permission is likely to be rescinded. . . . With this in mind, all national assignments will be shot in colour as of November 1.''

To operate within our assigned budget we would have to shoot considerably less colour film per story than we had black and white. And so I warned the staff, somewhat obscenely, that high public affairs film usage ratios – on the order of ten feet shot for every one used – were absolutely out. Four-to-one seemed like a nice round ratio. And so it was done, finally, but we'll never know how many feet of historic film, prior to the fall of 1970, were shot in black and white because of a preposterous Head Office, which looked after pennies with one hand and frittered away dollars with the other.

But in the fall of 1970, there were more serious things to occupy my mind than colour. There was the October Crisis, when the FLQ cell kidnapped James Cross, a British diplomat, and another grabbed Pierre Laporte, a Quebec cabinet minister. After invocation of the War Measures Act, the CBC over-reacted, and over-reacted badly. Taken in the context of the times, I suppose the CBC's response was understandable, if not entirely forgivable. Only a few Canadian voices were raised against the extremity of the government's actions against the FLQ, and except perhaps for an aggressive interview by one CBC reporter, Tim Ralfe, the CBC was not destined to be one of them.

The men in charge of the CBC at that time were products of the Second World War and the journalistic ethics and practices of that period. Our war correspondents, who had won the King's uniform, had been patriots first and journalists second. They had been heavily censored, and because they felt they were part of the war effort, merely chafed at the restrictions. That dimly remembered climate affected us all as late as 1970.

More important, perhaps, the management people who had most to do with the News Department's response were either new to management or new to journalism. What this meant was that journalistic principles were only faintly perceived by some, and the mechanics of defending those principles were not completely understood by others.

There was little warning. We were in the middle of it before we could come to grips with all its implications. As executive producer of the national news, I was called into the corner office of John Kerr, temporarily the head of News in the period following Joe Schlesinger's departure for the Hong Kong bureau. Kerr gave me my orders in tones of the utmost gravity. John was the colonel and I was the captain. It was the eve of battle, and we played our roles to the hilt.

At one point, I interrupted him. "What you're saying is that this is a matter of national security," I said.

"Yes," said Kerr. "Exactly."

I still have the empty cigarette pack on which I noted Kerr's instructions. We were to avoid commentary and speculation of all kinds. We were not to use man-on-the-street interviews or shoot film of any public demonstration. We were to air no panel discussions on the October Crisis and were to avoid reporting speculation, particularly speculation about what the government was doing. I was told, still in hushed tones, that the policy had been adopted by the highest levels within the corporation. In effect, I clicked my heels, saluted, and returned to duty.

Shortly after that, a message went out to news supervisors across the country, signed by C.K. Nash and John Kerr. Already, the corporation was rolling back a little. It read as follows:

"In view of the serious nature of events associated with the FLQ kidnappings we are requesting that special restraints be applied to all news and current affairs programmes dealing with these events or their implications.

"We must take special measures to avoid speculative stories.

"Our commentaries and discussions should be limited and each one must justify itself as a contribution to responsible programming.

"We cannot overemphasize the need for responsible editorial judgement at this time.

"If we have reservations about any story or commentary or analysis or discussions we must be prepared to kill it.

"Supervisors will implement this instruction immediately."

It was dated "Toronto, 9:40 P.M., October 15, 1970 (EDT)."

As I recall it, the cigarette-pack manifesto and the message that went out on the wire were rescinded within a matter of hours. Ironically, the usual roles were reversed. It was the CBC's legal staff who pointed out that we had over-reacted. I don't think any story was actually dropped because of the way Nash and Kerr's directions hit the panic button, but it would be a mistake to assume that no damage was done. It affected the CBC's coverage until the crisis was over.

The original directives were replaced by another, which simply forbad the broadcasting of raw FLQ propaganda, a restriction which was later abandoned by headquarters itself when, at gunpoint, the French network broadcast several of the FLQ's manifestos, without subsequent comment or any attempt to put them in any kind of editorial framework. But the original directives lived on, if not in letter then in spirit. They created a climate of timidity in which objective coverage of the October Crisis became almost impossible.

At 10:55 P.M. on October 15, the day that Nash and Kerr had their original attack of caution, a story clattered into the Toronto newsroom on the wires of Canadian Press that made me see red:

"Kidnap – CBC

"OTTAWA CP – George Davidson, president of the CBC, said Thursday [Oct. 15] he has told news departments of the French and English networks to reduce the amount of commentary devoted to the FLQ kidnappings of British diplomat James Cross and Quebec Labour Minister Pierre Laporte. Mr. Davidson said in an interview that certain parts of programs already planned would not be used and that other programs would be cancelled.

"He said the news media, including the CBC, have 'given far too much attention, particularly in the area of speculation,' to the kidnappings.

"The CBC news departments have been ordered to introduce 'more real, hard news' in place of commentary programs.

"He said a 'greater sense of accuracy in news and a greater discipline' were required.

"News coverage of the kidnappings, especially commentary, had 'gone farther than it is in the public interest that it should go,' the CBC president said.

"There had been 'instances of inaccuracies' in CBC coverage as well as in other reporting, and 'all sorts of wild rumours and speculation...

"'When you're playing with men's lives it's necessary to be somewhat more serious,' he said."

The night Pierre LaPorte's body was found, the CBC had broadcast false reports from a police source that the body of James Cross had also been located and because of a breakdown in communications, had continued to broadcast it for some time after it had been authoritatively denied.

"He said CBC executives had consulted government officials and cabinet ministers almost daily since the start of the kidnap crisis, but the 'decision we took was on our own responsibility.'

"Prime Minister Trudeau was not consulted on the specific decision to restrict coverage, Mr. Davidson said.

"'I have no idea what Mr. Trudeau's view is....'

"It was one thing to report such incidents in far-off countries but quite another 'when it's our own back yard,' he said.

"Decisions on just what will be covered by the CBC will remain with the heads of the news departments of the French and English networks. But they have been told to exercise 'more restraint as well as a measure of proportion' in broadcasting reports and comments on the kidnappings.

"The situation 'has reached the point where it has to be brought back into perspective,' Mr. Davidson said.

"Asked if CBC coverage of the kidnappings and related events had exceeded the real news values of the stories, he said that was 'a matter of judgement, and I'm in a position where that decision had to be made.'"

When I read the story, I was fit to be tied. In my view, Davidson was wrong about the historic importance of the story, and wrong in his perception of how it ought to be handled. The CBC president had used Canadian Press to criticize his own news service and what he said about what he wanted went far beyond, at least in tone, anything that had filtered down to us through our own supervisory channels.

When I had finished reading the story, I instructed Ron Collister, our chief Parliamentary correspondent, to take a camera crew, go to Davidson's home and interview him, despite the fact that it was after 11:00 P.M. Davidson refused to see him.

It seemed clear at the time that the over-reaction had begun with Davidson, whose background was the Civil Service, although a couple of months later, at a year-end meeting of the CBC's foreign correspondents in his Ottawa office, Davidson was at some pains to suggest that it was Nash who had been guilty of over-stepping the bounds. On the basis of the CP story, I found that hard to believe. Before Davidson had been made president of the CBC, he had had a reputation as one of the capital's best deputy-ministers. It was a reputation that didn't survive his years at the CBC.

I do not understand why we have not learned anything from the British experience. In Britain, the chairmen of both the BBC and the Independent Television Authority tend to exhibit the same kind of mandarinesque decision-making that has plagued the CBC. John Whale, in *The Half-Shut Eye*, notes that although the two chairmen have been traditionally impartial they have tended to exert their influence on the side of government in any dispute between Westminster and the broadcasters. He makes the point that this has not been out of political sympathy, but professional sympathy. As professional politicians and administrators in their previous experience, they have tended to understand government's problems better than those of their own industry or the man in the street.

A couple of weeks after my one-sided dispute with Davidson, I wrote a letter to Bill Bolt, the president of the Producers' Association, in which I recommended that some formal action be taken in connection with the Davidson interview and the instructions from Nash and Kerr. I noted that Davidson had been available to CP but not to us, argued that his philosophy was dangerous, and recounted the whole sorry collection of verbal and written restraining orders. And I mentioned the most recent and perhaps most alarming evidence of how far the corporation felt it had to go in keeping the ship of state on an even keel — the cancellation of a Tuesday-night program on Lenin, a dry, and I had been told somewhat dusty review of what was now ancient history, and which bore little if any relation to what was then happening in Canada. As far as I know, nothing came of the letter. I should have pursued it.

And that isn't the only regret I have about the October Crisis. I don't think there is much doubt that the air of caution, which by then hung over the place, affected me more than I realized. I recall watching a live remote feed from Ottawa one afternoon. Tim Ralfe, a member of the CBC's Ottawa bureau, was "door-stopping" the Prime Minister, who was due shortly at his Centre Block office.

When the Prime Minister came up the steps, Ralfe went for the jugular. It was an aggressive, hard-hitting interview, which for the first time revealed the extent of the Prime Minister's paranoia about the FLQ. When asked how far he would go with this thing (by this time there were armed soldiers on Parliament Hill), Trudeau suggested that Ralfe and the rest of us "just watch" him. That was the famous "bleeding hearts" interview.

I was furious, not about the Prime Minister's aggression but about Ralfe's. And in the heat of the moment, I bashed out a message to Ralfe on the Ottawa service wire, a teletype link with TV and radio news, in which I suggested that the next time he interviewed the Prime Minister, he should simply interview him. I said that the debate I had just watched being fed down from Ottawa defied every journalistic standard I had ever heard of.

The response came not from Ralfe, but from Angus McClellan, a senior radio news producer, then in Ottawa, who took me to task for using an open work wire for a personal reprimand. I had a fight with McClellan on the telephone and when I finally slammed down the receiver I was in no state to be making decisions. But I made one anyway. I ordered Bill Johnson, one of the news producers, to go down to Video Tape and do some editing. I wanted the most argumentative of Ralfe's questions eliminated. That is why, as far as I know, the only copy of that interview that still exists has in the middle of it a strange shot of the Peace Tower clock, the only "cutaway" Bill Johnson could find to avoid a "jump cut" when he edited out one of Ralfe's aggressive questions.

Needless to say, my relationship with Ralfe, which had long been uneasy on my side and openly contemptuous on his, was not improved. Very early on, thanks to the remonstrations of Peter Reilly, I began to have doubts about my treatment of him over the Trudeau interview. And so when I ran into Ralfe a couple of weeks later in the lobby of the Chateau Laurier in Ottawa, I tried to shake his hand. It was bad timing, to say the least. Ralfe told me to "fuck off," in a very loud voice. I am older and wiser now, and if that kind of thing happened today I would let it go.

But in those days, I had already begun to acquire the colouration of CBC management and I insisted that Ralfe be reprimanded. The reprimand went through, but the matter didn't end there. John Kerr, as head of News, had been hawkish about the Ralfe matter at the time of the Trudeau interview. He had fully endorsed my decision to have Bill Johnson cut it to ribbons. He had even expressed approval of my intemperate message to Ralfe on the work wire.

Six months later, probably due to pressure from the Guild, Kerr reviewed the reprimand, and, without consulting me, wrote a letter for Ralfe's file which effectively nullified the reprimand in any future assessment of his work. Second-guessing, at the CBC, was the standard order of business.

While the October Crisis was on, I was also in the middle of a stormy row with Michael Maclear, then our London correspondent. Maclear was one of the best reporters the CBC ever had, but he was also one of the most difficult. He was the bane of our harassed accountants, the same people who had learned to live with "piranha repellent." When it came to expense accounts, Maclear was royalty among mere nobility.

Because he was creative, knew his territory, and had a mind of his own, he was difficult to direct from the fifth floor. It was one of the unwritten rules of journalism that the man on the spot knows best, but there are times when those in charge of all the players on the board have to make dispositions with which not all of the players are in sympathy.

So it had been in September 1970, when trouble erupted in Jordan. Jordanian guerrillas, with the help of the Iraquis, were in a state of revolution, and for a time it seemed possible that they might be able to overwhelm the Jordanian forces loyal to the King. David Halton, who had been in Amman just before things came to a head, was by now in Beirut, sick, exhausted, and on his way home. Because Halton and his crew were in bad shape, and because he was returning to Toronto to do a crash special on Jordan, it made no sense to order him back in.

The nearest alternative on the board was Mike Maclear, who was then in Israel. So the decision was taken to move Maclear to Amman as quickly as possible. Maclear didn't say no, but he did erect a series of hurdles, which in the end had the same effect as an outright refusal.

During my first telephone conversation with Maclear, he objected to the assignment on the grounds that if the Jordanian guerrillas began to whip the King's army, the Israelis might be expected to take airborne action against them and the best story would be on the Israeli side. I disagreed with him because I didn't buy his scenario, and because even if I had, it would be much easier to get a replacement into Israel than it would to get another correspondent into Jordan. We hung up, still disagreeing.

Maclear called again about two hours later, and this time he was so negative about the possibility of getting into Jordan and connecting with a Current Affairs camera crew which was already there, that I asked him point blank if he were refusing to go.

Instead of answering the question, he asked me why I wouldn't use Barry Callaghan, a freelance contributor to CBC's weekend program, who was already there. I replied that, in my judgement, Callaghan was not suitable for daily news and that he, Maclear, was the best man for the job. Maclear said that I was talking "bull shit" and that the news service was just trying to save money. One of the sticking points was that Maclear had committed a cardinal sin when he arrived in Israel. Somehow, he had permitted the Israeli authorities to stamp his passport with an entry permit, instead of insisting on the time-honoured newsmen's practice of having a separate piece of paper stamped. A passport disfigured by an Israeli entry visa can't be used in Arab territory. And so, in any event, before he entered Jordan, Maclear was going to have to get a new passport, complicated by the fact that he was British. In the CBC's London office, Charlie Gunning had arranged for Maclear to come out as far as Athens, where a new passport was laid on. Maclear argued that the Arabs would be suspicious about a new passport issued in Athens and that the only way to avoid suspicion completely would be to come all the way out to London and have a new one issued there. Then he would go back to Beirut and get into Amman by the first available route.

In his second telephone call to me, Maclear pointed out that even if he were able to get the first available flight out of Tel Aviv to London, and he wasn't sure he could, he couldn't possibly be back in Beirut until a couple of days later. And he said he would go only on three conditions. One, he would expect the corporation to raise the insurance on his life to $200,000. ($100,000 was standard, at crippling war zone premiums. For example, it cost Global $5,000 to insure three of us for $100,000 in Vietnam for two weeks just prior to the fall of Saigon); two, it was to be understood that he would be flying to London first class and that he would also be flying first class from London to Beirut. (That was a standard bone of contention. The Correspondents' Association argued for, and later got, the right to first-class passage on long flights when work was scheduled to begin on the moment of disembarkation); three, he would have to have a "Telexed guarantee" that if the Arabs jumped him and held him hostage because he was a British citizen his full salary would continue to go to his wife during the period of imprisonment.

When I finally hung up after that conversation, I concluded that Maclear wasn't very keen to do the story and that it was going to take too long to bring him into play. And so, since speed is everything in television news, I began to look at the alternatives. Bill Cunningham, then the Hong Kong bureau chief, happened to be in Toronto cutting a film. And so we decided to move him into Beirut to stand by the first flight into Amman. He accepted the assignment and left immediately.

As it turned out, the Jordanian wrangle was the beginning of the end for Maclear at the CBC. I was angry, and I decided to leave him in Israel only until he wrapped up the immediate assignment. I then insisted that he be returned to London and kept there. I admitted his undoubted excellence as a correspondent, but made it clear to senior management and the assignment desk that as far as Macléar was concerned, London would be Coventry. I would refuse to talk to him or use him.

It was a ridiculous attitude with which to run a news service, complicated by the fact that Maclear did not report to me, which meant that I couldn't undo the decision. He was the property of Don MacDonald and Ron Robbins, in Editorial Resources. He had another boss too, in the person of Charlie Gunning, then the news supervisor in London. And, of course, all of the correspondents, because of the glamour of their jobs and the standing that gave them in the corporation, were free to deal directly with our superiors, Nash, Kerr, and the president himself.

Unfortunately for Maclear, it was John Kerr who took over the disposition of his case. Kerr was wearing two hats at the time, one as Nash's assistant – deputy director of Information Programming – and the other as temporary head of News. Kerr was blond, red-faced, and Roman Catholic. He was a tough-talking refugee from Current Affairs, with no hard news background, and a protégé of Marce Munro, the waspish assistant general manager of the English Services Division. In the early days, Kerr and I took our morning coffee breaks together. He had a fixation about the kind of sexual immorality that seemed to permeate the CBC, and it was often a topic of disapproving conversation at those morning breaks.

Despite Maclear's entreaties for a fair and impartial inquiry, and some written notice of the charges he was supposed to be facing, the situation was still unresolved by early January of 1971. The various executives who owned a piece of him were still arguing about what to do with him. By then I had come to believe that part of the problem had been a case of too many cooks, and perhaps also had come to realize that I couldn't run "The National" on successive fits of pique. I needed Maclear and I needed him badly.

I tried to convince Kerr that the overriding factor in our fumbling around with the Maclear case should be that despite the fact he was prickly, he was also one of the best men in the news service. And I added in a long memo:

"If that view were shared by all of us involved in the decision-making, I think we would be handling it somewhat differently. Be that as it may, I think the decision that now faces us is whether we want to keep Maclear or get rid of him. If, after all the pitches are made, we want to get rid of him, then I suggest we tell him so. If, on the other hand, we want to keep him, then I think we should tell him that too and govern our actions accordingly. I think that this whole thing ought to be cleared up and presented to Maclear this week."

Unfortunately, nothing at the CBC is that simple. I wanted Maclear as a national correspondent based in Toronto, on a salary sufficiently inflated over the standard rate so that it would not be an invitation to leave. I felt it would be good for Mike and good for us. I was still pushing that view vainly as late as May 11. No decision of any kind had yet been taken.

In the end, when Maclear had pretty well decided to go to CTV, I made the corporation's last pitch to him, unsuccessfully. It was our loss and CTV's gain. Eventually, what came out of Mike's defection was the half-hour series "Maclear," one of the most effective and popular information programs in the history of Canadian television.

While the Maclear crisis was still in full swing – some time during November – I was appointed head of News and Information Programming for the network, succeeding John Kerr, whose appointment had been temporary. I got a sad little note from Maclear, who was still languishing in London in the Coventry to which I had so foolishly sent him.

He had some flattering things to say, and added a warning:

"Only stay a programming man; stay in touch; go on encouraging collective achievement; a lot of people have put in a lot of years waiting and wanting to know that it was worth while. There's meaning to your job even beyond the product...."

He ended with some comments on his own situation, and a poignant little postscript: "But that's my story, Peter: it needn't be yours." I should have heeded Maclear's timely warning. I did pull back from programming and became more and more involved in the self-perpetuating corporate game. And I found, in the end, that I was an unimportant cog in a vast and mindless machine that was to grind on without me.

CHAPTER THREE

Management by Objective

When I took over as head of TV News, the corporation was in a state of upheaval. My title was head of TV News and Information Programming, but the only non-news program under my wing was "Viewpoint." I also had responsibility for the Toronto regional news operation. A decision had been taken to decentralize the CBC's English Services Division, and the skirmishing had begun as to how that policy would be put into effect. At the same time, an attempt was being made to rationalize the CBC's antediluvian management procedures, an objective close to the heart of Laurent Picard, then the CBC's executive vice-president, and Davidson's number two. Picard, all Harvard Business School, was horrified by the ramshackle structure he was supposed to work with. The CBC had grown like the average North American farmhouse. As it grew, a wing had been tacked on here, a woodshed added to the summer kitchen, and eventually, a toolshed had sprouted from the end of the woodshed. There was one essential difference between the CBC and the farmhouse, however. The farmhouse stopped growing when it got to be two or three times its original size. The CBC didn't. By the time Picard arrived on the scene, the CBC farmhouse had been expanded to cover the whole one-hundred-acre grant, and because of its scale, it had become an impossible, impassable labyrinth.

For me, trying to pick my way through this mess without shattering some corporate shibboleth became a full-time operation. I had some kind of control over "The National" newsroom, but none whatever over many of its components. As a result of the palace revolt that took place during the "Seven Days" crisis, News and Current Affairs had been joined in an uneasy marriage of convenience under Knowlton Nash as head of Information Programming. When "Seven Days" was in its glory, it became so powerful that, in terms of resources, it rivalled the news service. In fact, it had become what amounted to a second news service, going its own way, covering its own stories. Some duplication was absolutely necessary, of course. It would have been impossible for two program areas with separate mandates and looming deadlines to haggle in the screening rooms over who got what from each four-hundred-foot roll of newsfilm.

Surprisingly, perhaps, the deadlines for a weekly one-hour current affairs program are just as urgent as they are for a daily newscast. But there is no doubt that some resources could have, and should have been pooled. It would have helped to avoid the embarrassing display of CBC muscle at major events, where there could be four or more CBC TV crews: one shooting for "The National," another for the regional news, a third for "Seven Days," and perhaps one for "Newsmagazine." If it happened to be an event that fell into the bailiwick of one of the other Current Affairs program areas – religion or agriculture, for example – there could be as many as five or six crews.

The contrast between the hordes of CBC cameramen, soundmen, producers, correspondents, and story editors, and the lean manpower of CTV always looked bad in the papers. It always sounded worse than it really was in the hands of some ill-informed television critic intent on demonstrating how the CBC was wasting the taxpayers' money, because the critics rarely related the number of bodies to the amount of programming they produced. In any event, when management finally listened to the carping of its news division, and amalgamated News and Current Affairs under one administrative roof, it did not solve the old problems and the bitter News and Current Affairs rivalry went on as before. The feud continued because, in persuading the CBC to bring Current Affairs into the same unit, News failed to realize that it wouldn't have things all its own way, that Current Affairs might occasionally get precedence, and that News would have to surrender some of its autonomy. To deal with the old problem of duplication of resources, newsfilm cameramen, film editors, and other personnel were moved out of News into a separate area, a Resources division, which was designed to supply the needs of both News and Current Affairs. What this meant was that many of my key people reported to someone else. The graphic artists assigned to News already reported to the Graphics hierarchy in Sumach Street. The directors, script assistants, control room and studio crews who worked for News also reported to someone else – the technical and operations chief.

Under the amalgamation, we continued to lose not only key people, but key parts of the machine. "Newsmagazine," the unit responsible for its own weekly half-hour, and what we called "crash" specials – that is, in-depth programs hurriedly put together in the face of a developing story – was taken away from News and given its own executive producer. For a while, when Dick Neilson's Weekend programming was in full swing, the Saturday and Sunday newscasts were cut away from the weekday newscasts and given their own executive producer. In this instance, the division of authority began to mean that no one really controlled anything.

Another factor in the control problem was that the head of News had no authority whatever over the CBC's regional news operations. The Toronto region was an exception. But it was under the network news chief's wing because of the geographical accident rather than a corporate conviction that it was the only way to run a railroad. The regional news producers reported to the directors of their own particular regions, and this created a series of powerful, independent news fiefdoms right across the country. Unfortunately, there was no way to run a national news service without them.

It is true that we had our own national correspondents in each of the regions, reporters who worked solely for us, and who were on network strength. But they were almost completely dependent on the good offices of the regional producers for facilities, desk space, and much of their information. And because our own thin string of national correspondents couldn't possibly be responsible for every regional event of national importance, we were often dependent on the regional fiefdoms even for finished stories.

Even worse, for the long-term future of the service, we were effectively deprived of a farm system. There was no way we could feed promising young men and women into the bottom end, confident that they would get the right training and seasoning and eventually reach national stature. The standard in each region varied with the producers, and the jealousies that existed between them and the national service prevented useful co-operation in this area. To boot, the CBC's national training program, despite the fact that it involved some good people, was ineffective.

The main business of the fifth floor's corner office was not so much people, however, as their positions. Each department and each unit had a paper strength, that is, a fixed number of bodies or positions that had been frozen solid about the time of the last great ice age. As long as the magic number was not exceeded, you had a reasonable expectation of being able to get your people paid.

Thus, when Bernie Campin, the executive producer of the regional news, went back to radio, and took his position with him, I was furious. I'd not only lost Campin, but because of some kind of a deal that had been struck with radio without my knowledge, I'd also lost the right to replace him. And so filling vacancies and promoting people became not only a matter of weighing their qualities as professional individuals, but a complex, time-consuming chess game, in which we vainly tried to match our needs to our positions.

It was all supposed to save money, of course, but I'm not sure it really did in the end. If you had a reasonable argument in favour of it, you could convert a vacant copy clerk ''D'' position to a double ''A'' line-up editor's position. It would cost the corporation twice the money, but it had no effect on the news budget, since salaries were ''below the line'' charges and not our responsibility. As far as we were concerned, in the *lingua franca* of the CBC's budget officers, salaries were ''roubles.''

There were other anomalies in the staff regulations that made life difficult. A secretary's grade, which determines how much you can pay her, was derived from the position of her boss in the hierarchy. Thus, a busy junior grade manager, whose secretary might be required to function as more of an executive assistant, couldn't pay her as much money as the secretary of a senior manager whose own job might well be a sinecure, and whose secretary might spend two hours a day working and the other five filing her nails.

As head of network news, I spent something like $25,000 a week. Out of that came line and feed charges, raw filmstock and film processing, the payment of freelance cameramen, graphics, music, and things like war risk insurance. We did not, however, pay for studio facilities and crews, video tapes, or tape-editing time, or the cost of using a mobile on Parliament Hill. The end result was that our annual budget for what we called "above-the-line" costs, the budget for which we had responsibility and over which we exercised control, bore little relation to the real costs of the news service.

At that, it was a considerable budget. In 1970, when a dollar was still worth something, I spent close to $1,300,000. John Kerr, who was sitting in for Nash at the annual budget tribunal, gave me a hard time for coming in at $10,000 over budget, which even Dave Howard, the chief News accountant, felt was right on the money. As far as Howard was concerned, a $10,000 overage in a budget of $1.3 million, less than .8 per cent of the total, was something of an accomplishment.

There was a lot of waste inherent in that system of budgeting. For example, we couldn't make capital expenditures. So if we needed a piece of equipment, which the purchasing people didn't have the budget to supply, we had to lease it, and the result was that it cost the CBC its purchase price several times over.

One of the frustrations I didn't really need was "Viewpoint," the five or six minutes of individual opinion that followed a twenty-minute "National." Management had long been critical of the program. This was partly because the people who were supposed to have opinions tended to be amateur broadcasters, and often broadcast badly – partly because the opinions, particularly in the case of print journalists, were often thinly flavoured reports and not opinions at all, and partly because "The National" could have used that extra five minutes, and the money it cost. But no one could touch a hair on its head because "Viewpoint" had been the brainchild of Eugene Hallman, the vice-president of the English Services Division.

I've forgotten where the idea came from – it may have been mine, or it may have originated with someone else – but we decided finally that if we had to have "Viewpoint," it was time to make it more truly a voice of the people. Had resources been available, I would have turned it into a visual "letters to the editor." We would have continued to carry the reporter/expert "Viewpoint," reduced in length, and we would then have added to it several short film clips of viewers, reacting to both "Viewpoint" and events in the news. As it turned out, we simply couldn't free up the crews, the editing time, or the transmission and recording facilities to do it. "Viewpoint's" facilities were already being stretched to the breaking point. So we decided to do the next best thing: give "Viewpoint" a host, who would introduce that night's opinion, and then read a selection of letters from viewers. It wasn't the most exciting program concept, but it seemed to me that it met some of the objections to the existing version of "Viewpoint," and it had the added advantage of giving the CBC's ordinary viewers, for the first time, some limited access to the airwaves.

I hadn't reckoned with Eugene Hallman. I'll never forget the area heads' meeting, which the vice-president attended to make his views known on the projected violation of his pet concept. To say the least, he was disturbed, and he all but decreed that we should leave it alone. Almost as if I hadn't heard him, I told the area heads what it was we were going to do. I wouldn't say that there were sharp intakes of breath around the conference table, but there was a nervous stillness as I outlined the new format for "Viewpoint" as if it were a *fait accompli*. Hallman was silent too.

A happy result of the new format was that I was able to get "old stone-face," Earl Cameron, back on the air in a late-night slot immediately after his old assignment, "The National." I was pleased by it, Earl was, and thousands of viewers were too.

One of the headaches that "Viewpoint" caused in both the old format and the new had to do with the fact that because it was a CBC program, and because it solicited a broad range of informed opinion, some people felt they had a right to appear. It paid only a modest fee, never more than $100 in my memory, so this conviction apparently had more to do with the prestige of the platform than a desire to share the gravy.

On one occasion, Eugene Hallman got a letter from a well-known man about the media who equated his right to appear on "Viewpoint" with the right to vote. He demanded to know whom to contact, what the policy was, and whether a fee was paid. Hallman passed the letter to me for a reply. When I had answered the gentleman's questions, I felt it necessary to add:

"I can't believe that you are serious about there being an avenue for 'appeal' in the event that a request for exposure is denied. 'Viewpoint' is a CBC Television production, not the Supreme Court. Pure program judgements, which do not run afoul of CBC policy, are the producer's prerogative."

Perhaps I should have added "at least on paper." In news, the producer's prerogative, even the area head's prerogative, was pretty well confined to the disposition of paper clips.

Knowlton Nash is an old friend. I first met him in the late fifties or early sixties when I was the UN correspondent for the *Montreal Star*. We didn't get to know each other well until some time after I moved to Washington in 1962. I think it's fair to say that Knowlton knew almost everyone, but was close to very few, and most of them were business associates.

Knowlton was still the Washington correspondent in 1968, when I was hired as an editor "C" for "The National." As I mentioned earlier, he played an active role in getting me and the CBC together. He had considerable clout during that period, because he was about to head the marriage between News and Current Affairs as head of Information Programming.

When he moved into the new job, it was a bit difficult for both of us. We had remained friends during the intervening years, and he and his wife Sylvia had often been our house guests when CBC business brought Knowlton to Ottawa. I was always amused by the way Knowlton, even as a correspondent, played the corporate game. He seemed to be almost totally a political animal, wheeling and dealing within the CBC. His telephone bills must have been enormous. He was an active part of the cabal that had been trying to reshape CBC News since 1966. The problems that I was to encounter as an executive producer and then area head, between 1969 and 1971, were old ones. The fifth floor had long been a boneyard for the passions and dreams of the people who cared most about the news service.

Bill Cunningham was the sparkplug of the reform movement. As executive producer of "The National" in 1966, Cunningham put his convictions and those of key people like Nash into a memorandum which proposed nothing less than a revolution.

Then as now, news was Cunningham's religion. He has little time for anything that is not directly related to the business. He wanted CBC News to be more thoughtful, penetrating, and original. He wanted no more of the good grey newscast that sounded like CP's Broadcast News wire, but with dignity. He wanted the assignment desk to originate news, not merely to react to CP and the Toronto newspapers. He wanted the other medium to pursue and credit the CBC. He wanted the CBC News to have the prestige of an electronic *New York Times,* and he knew that to achieve that, the CBC web would have to be untangled and that he would have to hire a lot of good new people.

"We want to be the common reference point for all that is news in this country and beyond," he said in the definitive memo. "We want to be the one source to which all Canadians turn for the right information – not just accurate information, but skilful and perceptive interpretation of what has happened, what is happening and what will happen. We want the newspapers and the magazines and the wire service to follow us. We want them to quote us because we get the story first, we get it accurately, and we understand its deeper implications."

Cunningham's proposals were detailed (the general presentation covered fifty-three legal-size pages) but the key elements were relatively simple. Like others in the news service, he saw the overlap in manpower and facilities between News and Current

Affairs as a crippling drain in the corporation's resources. He wanted to end the destructive rivalry between them.

He believed that this could be accomplished with the creation of a two-man News and Current (or Public) Affairs vice-presidency, the division of responsibility to be between the English and French networks, not News and Current Affairs. In the English network, this would have had the effect of putting News and Current Affairs in both TV and radio, and network and regional news organizations under one powerful roof. It would have, for the first time, co-ordinated radio and TV news, and would have given the vice-president and his general manager clear-cut authority over the regional news fiefdoms.

Cunningham also wanted to bring all the independent components of the news service – film cameramen, soundmen and film editors, graphic artists and a set designer, directors and script assistants, technical producers and floor directors – into the news establishment. He wanted to build a news studio as an integral part of the newsroom on the fifth floor. And central to the whole thrust of his demands was that the CBC resolve the problems between the announcers' union and the editorial union, and clear the way for real news anchormen, in the American sense, what he called "announcer-reporters," who would be involved in the gathering, assigning, writing, and delivery of the news. For Cunningham, that was the nub. Everything else tended to be mere window dressing, unless there was a resolution of this central issue.

"It is vital," he wrote in his report, "to the success of this program, and indeed to the whole of the news service, that the man up front reporting the news, be a man of the right qualifications. These qualifications must be such that he is able to take not just a part in the preparation of the program, but a leading part. To all who watch and listen, he must appear to be the complete master of all he holds.... To the public, he will be the CBC News, and to satisfy it, he must be capable of personally covering and reporting major events in this country."

To Cunningham, the credibility of the news service had to begin with the anchorman. Even then, in the sixties, he sensed the public's growing suspicion of the media, and he felt strongly that

CBC News would have no hope of dealing with that suspicion unless the man who fronted the news knew what he was talking about and believed it. What Cunningham called the "news actors," the announcer-readers, had served the CBC "honourably and faithfully," but in his view, their day was over.

It wasn't just Cunningham who had a bee in his bonnet about the anchorman's role, although he was considerably ahead of his time. Ray Hazzan, Cunningham's boss, fully endorsed his sentiments on that subject and most of the others:

"We recommend acceptance of the principle that working newsmen host all news programs," Hazzan wrote in a companion memo. "We can no longer be satisfied with the use of announcers to read newscasts in which they have no involvement. The credibility and integrity of the news can only be enhanced if the man who presents it to the public has had a hand in gathering and preparing it."

Thirteen years later, that principle has still to be accepted by the CBC, and a member of the Cunningham group which based its fight on that principle, Knowlton Nash, is now the victim of the corporation's inactivity.

Some of the suggestions contained in the Cunningham report were adopted by the CBC. But the important principles, that there be a vice-president of News and Current Affairs, and that the man who reads the news be a newsman, were all but ignored. News and Current Affairs were pulled together, in a fashion, and shoved under the same roof, for a short period, with radio news. But the man at the apex of the roof was only a director, not a vice-president, and the man who was appointed director, Knowlton Nash, had neither the clout nor, it seemed, the desire to make the Cunningham vision come true.

Cunningham did get his man to read the news; Stanley Burke, a man with all the right qualifications. But because of the unresolved union dispute, he was given no chance to exercise his considerable gifts as a correspondent, except during news specials. He was capable, but not able, because to take the job he had to join the announcers' union, and in that situation he had no more latitude than his announcer predecessors.

Weary from the struggle, Cunningham wound up in a hospital bed, and was fired as executive producer before he became an out-patient. When he recovered, he was sent to Asia, to man the Hong Kong bureau and cover the Vietnam war.

At home, the internal war went on. Joe Schlesinger continued the struggle as the new executive producer, and Nash, when he later headed information programs, took up one or two of Cunningham's old cudgels. He wielded at least one of them to some effect, and won the so-called "electronic highway." But in some of the skirmishes, he seemed to lose sight of the war. Under Nash, the amalgamation of News and Current Affairs meant that News increasingly lost control over its own destiny. This was obvious even to the Current Affairs side in the new arrangement. When John Kerr, after his brief stint as head of News, returned full time to his job as Nash's deputy and the unofficial representation of the Current Affairs half of the union, he warned Nash that the continuing erosion of News control over its own elements was a fundamental error.

Kerr referred specifically to the Information Resources unit, to which foreign correspondents, film editors, and a host of other news people reported. In a memo to Nash, he noted that the contradictions in the system were leading to "confusion of lines, low morale, and inevitably to frictions that could be avoided... It seems to me quite unacceptable that one supervisor should be responsible for personnel when he is not responsible for their product."

The word "unacceptable" was the strongest in Kerr's lexicon of condemnation. There were other words in mine, and I found myself resorting to them more and more frequently. I seethed through gritted teeth at the daily noon meetings in Nash's office, and when they came ungritted, Nash fanned the flames by operating on the principle that a bland answer turneth away wrath. I got angrier and angrier.

Even standing still was a tortuous process at the CBC. When we had a vacancy to fill, it often took months before we could move the appropriate paper through the labyrinth of offices that had a hand in hiring and firing, and "post" it, that is, actively and officially solicit applications. On one occasion, when I found myself with seven open positions for which I had been unable to get paper moving, I wrote to Don MacDonald, the general supervisor of Information Resources, in a last, desperate effort to unplug the system. I felt it necessary to carbon copy eight of the other people involved. I don't remember whether or not it worked, but I would be willing to bet that I didn't get more than three of the seven positions opened up in the month that followed.

Nash was not the originator of the CBC's organizational problems, but in my time he did very little to solve them, and he himself became something of a burden. When he finally made it out of the ranks of the Correspondents' Association and into senior management, it was as if a dam had burst. You got the impression that he enjoyed the trappings of management as much as the substance. When I was promoted into management myself, I discovered that Nash, who had once conducted virtually all of his business on the telephone, had instead become addicted to memos. They flew out of his Kremlin office like flakes in a snowstorm. On any given day, there were from three to a dozen new Nash memos on my desk, some of them simply drawing my attention to an attached newspaper or periodical clipping, others requiring exhaustive research or much soul-searching. It was disconcerting when you were in the middle of trying to get one more newscast on the air to get a memo from Nash requiring all of your suggestions for news programming five years down the road. Or one that required that you compose a civil reply to a Member of Parliament who complained that "The National" was dull and needed pacing.

It was bad enough having to read the memos. But Nash had become so ruthlessly bureaucratic in a short time that you had to reply to them fairly quickly. He and his capable secretary had a foolproof listing system which meant that any memo that went without a response for what seemed like a very short time automatically drew a follow-up memo, often in peremptory tones, demanding to know why one hadn't responded to the memo of such and such a date on a matter of considerable national urgency.

From the Hong Kong bureau and the relative safety of Vietnam, Cunningham watched and waited. Gradually, he became incensed with Nash's performance, on which he had pinned his hopes for the revitalization of the news service. Rightly or wrongly, he came to view Nash as a traitor to the spirit of '66, and he has never forgiven him for it.

It was in the middle of my wrestling match with Nash and the system that executive vice-president Laurent Picard released his shock troops from the Harvard School of Business. The decision had already been taken to decentralize the English Services Division. The rationale seemed to be that Ontario wasn't Canada, and that if more and more programming originated in the regions, the CBC would better inform Canadians about what the rest of the country was really like. It was a rationale I disputed, particularly as it applied to network news.

But when Picard threatened to streamline decision-making, and make management practices conform to what it was we were trying to do, despite my misgivings, I accepted his call to arms with a reasonably open mind. The vice-president staged a series of senior management seminars at what had been the old Seigneury Club at Montebello, Quebec. Several groups of twenty-five or thirty people took the five-day management course during the summer of 1969.

It sounded good on paper. The elements of the corporation's management philosophy to be discussed were:

"Decentralization of decision-making.

"Management by objectives.

"Responsibility and authority delegated to the level directly concerned with the activity.

"Accountability by managers for the results of decisions and actions.

"Implementation of a management information system (MIS) to serve the needs of the corporation for management and operational data."

While I read the prospectus, I detected the stirring of cautious enthusiasm. But when I got to Montebello, and got stuck into the lectures, the old gloom began descending. I had no difficulty seeing how those systems might work for the Bank of Commerce, or even for CTV. But I had trouble relating them to the CBC, and even more difficulty relating them to the national news.

Who was going to tell Nash that "responsibility and authority" should be "delegated to the level directly concerned with the activity?" I was willing, but was John Kerr willing? For that matter, was Joe Schlesinger? When I sought some kind of practical direction, I was fobbed off with business school double-talk. I was told that "News is a sub-activity of a sub-program." Program, in that sense, of course, had nothing to do with a television program. And neither, as it turned out, did the five-day Montebello seminar.

The one thing I did get out of the course was some idea of the concept of management by objective. What this meant, as nearly as I could discover, was that having determined an objective, you then set down, with all the individual pros and cons, the alternative routes that were available to reach that objective. I used the system to good effect in my last major presentation to CBC management. Everything went swimmingly, except that Nash and company wouldn't buy the objectives. Somehow, I was right back where I had started.

The only time I met Laurent Picard was when he addressed one of those Montebello sessions. He was an impressive figure, full of himself, full of the wisdom of the course of action he was proposing. He gave the impression of rapid movement and enormous energy.

But as I remember his lecture, the problem was that he kept relating the CBC to General Motors. With GM, for example, it had been a "marketing based" decentralization. The CBC's decentralization would be "technology based." And by the time he got to our union situation ("Walter Reuther has never negotiated how a car is going to be made"), I knew we were in for it. I was tempted to suggest that Picard negotiate the next contract with the Guild. He would soon find out that Gerry MacDonald not only wanted to negotiate how the car was made but to redesign the thing too.

When Picard rationalized the reasons for the disastrous CBC producers' strike as "high centralization at the top and a highly decentralized production level imposed by the nature of the technology," I knew that as far as the CBC was concerned, he was talking through his toque. He had reduced things to a formula, but the formula would never be made to work.

I had one more contact with Picard as executive v-p, although this time it was second-hand. A newsroom employee of some fourteen years' standing swore at a supervisor and left in the middle of his shift. In some places it might have been cause for dismissal. But not at the CBC.

I opted for a reprimand, which was approved by the CBC's industrial relations people and sent by registered mail to the employee's home. A reprimand, in CBC terms, is a letter expressing a supervisor's dissatisfaction, a copy of which is placed on the employee's permanent file, where it is considered, with the rest of the file's contents, in the event of promotion or dismissal.

The shop steward and the unit chairman decided to fight the reprimand on the employee's behalf, and their opening gun was a letter to me, with copies to Industrial Relations and Laurent Picard. The gist of their letter was that the employee in question was ill at the time he had walked out and that he was currently receiving medical treatment. But after he came back to work, the employee in question had refused some newsroom chore with a grin and the remark that "I'm supposed to be sick," so I was not disposed to put much stock in the theory that he was being disciplined, as the letter put it, "for displaying the symptoms of his illness in an unseemly fashion."

I was even less inclined to reconsider the reprimand when I read on and discovered that the man's trade union brothers were not above using a little blackmail to get the matter dropped.

"We have had several recent cases of nervous and emotional breakdown in the newsroom," the letter continued, "and in no case was disciplinary action taken against the person involved.

"One particular case involved an employee who had a problem with alcohol. In this instance, he had returned to the newsroom in a drunken condition after a considerable absence and, in front of the entire staff, confronted the manager of Regional News and threatened to 'puke on his head.' No disciplinary action was instituted in this case, nor did this employee's action inhibit his advancement within the corporation, since he has now become a member of management.''

Those of you who have read the first chapter about life in the zoo, may recognize the employee ''in a drunken condition'' as me. It wasn't an entirely fair comparison, because I had been off-duty at the time, and the next day, when I pieced together what had happened, I apologized to the man in question, who was a hard-working and altogether inoffensive individual.

But the letter containing the veiled charge had gone not just to me, but to Laurent Picard and Industrial Relations, and there wasn't much doubt about what the union's next move would be if I didn't back off.

So I wrote a letter to the union, with copies to Industrial Relations (one of which I ordered to be placed on my own file) and to the vice-president. In it, I confessed to the crime described (pointing out that I had been off-duty and that I had apologized), and warned the union that because I now knew something about problems with alcohol, I would, for the sake of any employee who developed the problem, deal strictly with any subsequent drunkenness in the newsroom. I made the point that the corporation did an employee no favour in ignoring problems with alcohol, a comment that should have made some impression on the addressees, both of whom had been known to take a drink. And I flatly refused to reconsider the reprimand. It was a touch righteous, perhaps, but I did it with feeling. And in any other organization, it would have been case closed.

But not at the CBC. The union went behind my back with impunity. There were further letters, telephone calls, and perhaps even meetings between the union and the vice-president, with no further reference to me. The first I knew about all of this came through a request to meet with a senior television official in the Kremlin. He gave me the background, and advised me to drop the reprimand. He revealed that there had been further exchanges between the union and Picard, and that Picard, perhaps on the basis of his perception of Walter Reuther, rather fancied himself as an expert in the field of labour-management relations.

I don't know to this day whether the executive played up to me because he thought I was a tough disciplinarian, or whether he really believed the philosophy he espoused. But he admitted that he too, in his time, had had difficulty "getting" certain of his employees. He described, with real or pretended glee, how he had stalked one miscreant for months until he finally caught him in a violation and fired him for keeps, with the full weight of the CBC staff manual behind him. I left his office feeling slightly sick. I don't know whether the reprimand was lifted or not. At that stage, I wasn't particularly interested.

The only warm feeling I have in connection with that incident is for Nash, who came through when it counted. He had read the exchange of correspondence, of course, and noted in a memo I value that "it is greatly to your credit to have handled the matter in the way you have."

The true state of staff relations in the newsroom is revealed to some extent by my own brush with blackmail. Feelings were running high and they tended to be venomous. We were unable to use one of our most senior and highly paid reporters with any frequency, because of his drinking. In my view, the CBC was as much to blame as the individual. There had never been any serious attempt to make him face his problem or deal with it effectively. I found myself caught in the middle again when a member of the regional news staff had managed something of a first for the dark days of the early seventies. He'd managed to get pubic hair on the screen, quite unnecessarily in my view, in the middle of a regional news item. He felt that I was a contemptible prude for not seeing it his way. I wanted to reprimand him, but in this instance, the same senior management who viewed blackmail with equanimity, wanted him fired. I had to fight them off from two directions.

Meanwhile, there was a faction in the newsroom which was actively working to sabotage the best efforts of one of our best correspondents, in Washington, and he was about ready to quit. One of our freelance cameramen, who we paid an enormous annual fee for those days, hadn't paid his own soundman for six months. Legally, there was nothing we could do about it. Morally, we had to do something.

A news producer, whom I had asked to carry out specific duties in the newsroom, flatly refused sometime after he'd left for vacation. I got the refusal on the back of a picture postcard, mailed from his holiday retreat. I was also in the middle of some gentle jousting with Ron Collister, of the Ottawa bureau, who thought I wanted to get rid of him because of his English accent. I had it on good authority that he was prepared to have the matter raised as a civil rights issue in the House. I didn't want to get rid of him. I wanted him reassigned, and the Liverpool lilt with the Canadian overtones was only part of the reason. I didn't like Maclear's accent either, not because I don't like the English, but because enough was enough on Canada's national news. But I didn't want to reassign Maclear, because Maclear was a genius with film. Certainly at that time, Collister had never learned to use film skilfully, something I felt had to be construed as a defect in a television reporter.

The day-to-day problems were endless, but I saw an outlet for some of my frustrations when a committee, headed by Hallman's special assistant, Peter Herndorff, asked me, Don Cameron, the executive producer of Regional TV News, and Don MacDonald, the general supervisor of Information Resources, to come up with a plan for the decentralization decision in the news area.

I saw this not as an opportunity for a stand against decentralization, because that had long since been decided at levels far removed from ours, but as a chance to regain some of our lost autonomy in the ensuing turmoil. If we had to take a step backwards with decentralization, perhaps we could take three steps forward at the same time. And so the three of us deputized our number-two people to run things in our absence, and for a week we cleared out of our offices and debated it all in seclusion.

What we decided in the end was that in Toronto, the national and regional operations should be physically separated in such a way that it would give both areas improved facilities. That was the step backwards, putting the Toronto region on the same footing as all the other regional newsrooms: It was hard to swallow, because many of the news service's most serious problems, as I have already described them, stemmed directly from the split between the network barons and the news squires in the regions.

But we also recommended that the Information Resources unit, which owned a lot of the news service's raw talent, should be broken up, and the key bodies returned to the newsroom. Don MacDonald very generously supported this position, for the good of the news service, despite the fact that it would have cost him his standing as an area head and would have made him my deputy.

We recommended that "crash" specials should be moved back into news where they belonged. And we urged strongly that the news area head be in a position to act as a mentor to the regional news operations, giving them strong professional guidance in matters of news policy, editorial and production standards, and staff development and training. To give this diplomatic role some teeth, we suggested that the news area head should be consulted closely in the appointment of regional news supervisors. Who knows, it might have been enough to start putting Humpty-Dumpty back together again.

Despite our painful awareness of the ways of the corporation (and Cameron's and MacDonald's longer service had made them even more aware than I was) we were confident that senior management could not fail to heed the recommendations of the three senior people in the news service.

We delivered the report to Nash personally, several days before he was due to leave on vacation. We left him in no doubt that we regarded the recommendations as vital to the future of the service, and that the steps we had suggested should be adopted quickly. I didn't hear from Nash again until after he'd gone on leave. He had physically left the office, but his memos were still spewing methodically out of his dictating machine, and I finally got a curt little note from him, signed by his secretary. The note said that our precious report had been turned over to Peter Campbell, the general supervisor of program policy and planning, and Ross McLean, still with time on his hands as a special consultant. Neither of them had any particular expertise in news, and although they were both good fellows, the thought of alien corporate paws on what for the three of us had been a last, desperate effort to make sense, was simply too much for me to have to bear.

On June 15, 1971, I sent Nash a confidential cable care of Charlie Gunning, the news supervisor in London:

"Sorry Knowlton," it read. "Peter Campbell and Ross McLean too much. I am resigning from the corporation effective August 1. My decision is not negotiable. Cheers etc. . . ."

The tragedy is that I don't think Knowlton ever really understood what I was upset about. He had become such a bureaucrat that he could see nothing wrong in cavalierly handing our report to two more bureaucrats for more evaluation. If he had said to us before he left, "Look, I agree with much of what you've said, but I'm not sure of all the implications, and I'd like some other opinions on what it might mean to other program areas," I think we'd have understood Campbell and McLean.

In a memo dated a month later, I tried to explain myself to Nash, and tried to ensure that I hadn't irreparably damaged our long-standing personal relationship.

"I felt and continue to feel that unless I was given a completely free hand with what is left of the news service, I was going to have to stand by helpless and watch it go down the drain. I don't think you have realized how deeply the rot has set in, Knowlt, or have realized that my chief value to you was my own news judgement, exercised without the encumbrance of second guesses by John Kerr, Laurent Picard, Norn Garriock, Marce Munro, Eugene Hallman, or on occasion, by CKN [C. Knowlton Nash]. . .

"I feel that leadership of the CBC is second or third rate from George Davidson on down, and that unless the corporation gears itself to quality information programming, and that kind of priority alone (with a much greater set of priorities for news) the Government of Canada is very soon going to find that the annual appropriation is much too high, and that the country should contemplate trying to get along without the CBC in anything resembling its present form. . . ."

So much for my prescience. The corporation's budget has doubled or tripled since 1971, and although the rumbling continues to be heard from the committee rooms of Parliament Hill, no concerted effort has yet been made to rationalize CBC operations, or ensure that the taxpayer gets value for money spent.

It wasn't my last memo to Nash or my last encounter with the CBC. Shortly before I left, five of us from radio and TV news met to discuss an appointment to the Ottawa bureau to replace Tom Earle, who was being moved to London. I pointed out to Nash that we couldn't shape the bureau the way we wanted because of the Ottawa "star" problems which had haunted us since the days of Norman DePoe. Once assigned to the bureau, its members built up too much influence on Parliament Hill. They were close to the politicians, and to CBC headquarters in Ottawa South. The five people who had met in good faith in Toronto couldn't even be sure that the appointment they agreed on could be made to stick. Someone senior, knowing nothing of the news service's requirements, could well veto the decision for some reason that had nothing whatever to do with news, but CBC politics.

"Your shrugging your shoulders and pointing out that you couldn't decide on correspondents either doesn't help, I'm afraid," I wrote Nash. "Because you aren't going to resign in the belief that this should be the news area head's decision or even your own. How in the name of all that's holy, knowing that, can I explain to you why I'm resigning?... There was so much I couldn't do as news area head, beyond carrying messages, that there just wasn't any job. So all I've really done is moved from the ranks of the jobless to the unemployed."

Like most CBC expatriates, I was bitter and continue to be. In the intervening years, I have often wondered if I hadn't exaggerated the impossibility of rational action at the CBC. But when I left, Bill Cunningham came back from London to take my place, and gave up in disgust himself in less than a year.

And in having to retrace my steps while writing this book I have concluded that it was at least as bad as I had remembered and perhaps, face to face with the collected frustrations, even worse.

No one realizes better than I do that I might have accomplished something if I had stayed to play the corporate game. I was an uneven administrator, an erratic leader, and young enough to think I wasn't. It gives me no pleasure to put all of this on paper, but I think the people who pay the bills deserve to know what we were up against.

CHAPTER FOUR

The Anchormen

The word "anchorman" does not appear in the shorter Oxford Dictionary. For one thing, the Oxford is slow to accept the realities of linguistic change; for another, there are no anchormen, in the television news sense, in England. And there are very few real anchormen in this country either. But the word "anchor" does appear in the Oxford, of course, and its secondary meaning gives us a clue to the function of the anchorman in North American terms. An "anchor" is described as "that which gives stability or security."

It seems obvious to me that the host of a newscast cannot supply stability or security for the time he has to fill if all he does is read a script that someone else has written, arranged, and handed to him. All you need for that is boyish good looks, a cat-gut larynx, a carefully modulated voice, and enough wit to read with reasonably appropriate emphasis. You hear people like that on private radio every day of the week. They often seem to be more preoccupied with the timbre of their voices than what they're using them for. They talk the same way on and off duty, and if you've ever stood behind a radio announcer in the corner grocery store, and heard one of those fat, rich radio voices asking carefully for a pound of coffee as if they were doing a station break, you know what I mean.

It is a natural enough phenomenon. An announcer's or a news-reader's voice, his projection, his pronunciation, is the main item of business. If you have been freed from writing the news yourself, you tend to be occupied more with performance than substance. Writing is someone else's job. Your job is delivery. But this division of responsibility can have an unfortunate side effect, and sometimes one hears an announcer delivering the details of a tragedy in the same sprightly, well-rounded tones that he has just used to relay the weather. He's not feeling the story. Odd as it may seem, he may not even be aware of the details.

Ted Baxter, the prototype announcer on the "Mary Tyler Moore Show," was asked after a newscast one night about the name of a man whose death he had described, or something of that order.

"I don't know," replied Baxter. "I wasn't listening."

That line has probably drawn millions of laughs in endless reruns of the "Mary Tyler Moore Show" on several continents, but it isn't really funny. You can read a newscast without listening. I know. I read a weather forecast every night, and if you ask me when it's over what the weather's going to be I can't tell you. I don't write the weather, I'm not particularly interested, and I handle that part of the newscast mechanically. I don't listen.

I had always rather fancied myself as a pundit, anchorman, or some other kind of broadcast father figure from the first time I heard my German professor's reverential tones when she talked about Edward R. Murrow instead of Schiller or Goethe. But until Bill Cunningham was struck by the same notion, it had been an unlikely dream.

When I quit the CBC as head of News in 1971, Cunningham replaced me. Somehow, between them, he and Don Cameron made me forget the nightmare I had lived on the fifth floor, and persuaded me to return to the CBC, this time as a reporter for Cameron's regional news. It meant joining the Guild again and working shoulder to shoulder with people for whom I had been, only a few months before, a fairly tough boss. But in the end, the prospect of filling in a gap, of learning something about television news that had so far eluded me, that is, television news reporting, was too strong to resist. I had known what sort of reporting I wanted, and what I liked, but like most critics, I didn't know how to do it. As it turned out, there was surprisingly little friction with my one-time employees, my new colleagues.

Cunningham had sweetened the pot, of course. Not with money this time, but with prospects. The understanding was that if I learned to work with film, and could become a competent television reporter, my fifteen years as a newspaper reporter, foreign correspondent, and columnist would then be reason enough to give me one of the CBC's overseas bureaus.

Less than a year later, my prospects went down the drain when, after one more attempt to reform CBC News, Cunningham quit. Recognizing the CBC's inability to take its own experts seriously, Cunningham had commissioned Brian Nolan to study CBC News, take it apart, and make recommendations. Nolan's credentials were impressive. He had helped to design CTV's first national newscast, when it came out of Ottawa. He had worked for "Seven Days," and he had worked for ABC as a senior producer in New York, Washington, and London. He was a Canadian with American network clout.

Nolan made it clear to Cunningham, before they started, that he would come to his own conclusions, and that once the study began, Cunningham should butt out. Cunningham accepted the conditions with confidence because he knew Nolan was a professional, and that no serious news producer could fail to share many of his own views.

So it turned out. Nolan presented the corporation with a six-volume report on the news service, and some 200 recommendations.

"I agreed with every one of the two hundred recommendations," Cunningham recalls. Nolan's report had been very much in the spirit of his own '66 manifesto. Nolan wanted increased funding, updated facilities, electronic news gathering (ENG), an open newsroom, the development of broadcast journalists and real anchormen.

The Nolan report sat in the Kremlin for a week, without a meaningful response. Cunningham pushed for agreement on something, anything, as a token of good faith. Nash and company wouldn't agree to a single one of the 200 recommendations, so Cunningham resigned.

Ironically, his resignation paved the way for reform. When Denis Harvey took over, much of the Nolan report was finally implemented; all except the provision that the man who reads the news should be a working journalist. Harvey apparently didn't think that was important.

Cunningham moved to CTV for a time, and took over "W-5." But when Al Bruner got a licence for the new Ontario network, he saw the possibilities. When the job of heading Global's news service was finally offered, Cunningham, in effect, demanded and got a vehicle for the recommendations he'd been pushing at the CBC since 1966. He became the first vice-president for news in a Canadian network. Shortly afterwards, CTV followed suit, making its News and Current Affairs chief, Tom Gould, the first News vice-president at that network.

Cunningham also got Global to agree to a number of important principles, not the least of which was that anchormen should be working journalists, writing their own newscasts and their own comments, and reporting often enough to keep their credentials renewed.

Cunningham tried to get a number of high-profile newsmen as anchormen, unsuccessfully. He ran into considerable reluctance because of the obvious risks involved in tying one's professional wagon to a new and untried regional network.

He rescued me from the CBC in the spring of 1973, several months before Global was due to go on the air. I was to be a roving foreign correspondent, based in Toronto. In the meantime, that first summer I worked for Brian Nolan, hosting, writing, and producing a series of half-hour documentaries called "Global News Journal," destined to be the news service's first current affairs program. I shot the first foot of Global film, on the first foreign assignment, in London that summer, and it would be pointless to deny that while I was doing it, I had a strong sense of history-in-the-making. I shot four European films in the space of a month, returned to Canada and cut them in Ottawa. By the time I had started to edit four additional Canadian films for the "Journal" series, Cunningham was running out of choices for anchormen. I think he had pretty well decided that Peter Desbarats, who had been hired as Ottawa bureau chief, could do the job for him.

In any case, Cunningham booked a studio and facilities at the CTV outlet in Ottawa, to give Desbarats a dry run at an ABC news script. I was editing a "Journal" on our national capital that afternoon, and Cunningham asked me to come to the studio too. Nolan was furious that Cunningham had winkled me away from half a day's editing, and I never heard the end of it. On our way to the studio, Cunningham explained to me that he was thinking of using me now and then as a back-up anchorman, and he simply wanted to see what I looked like in that role.

For some reason or other, I was in an aggressive mood when the camera light winked on and I was given my cue. I had just watched Desbarats do his number, and for my money, he had been a little too genteel. And so I stormed into the script, news pouring out of me like smoke.

When it was over, Cunningham was pleasantly shaken, and for the first time he began talking about two anchormen, me in Toronto, Desbarats in Ottawa – the old Huntley-Brinkley routine. I suspected he had typecast me as Brinkley – a little sour, a bit odd looking. I was wrong. It was Huntley he had in mind when he screened the audition.

It was the last thing anyone else had in mind when Global News finally went on the air. We had been in dry runs for a month before we went on the air on January 7, 1974, but we had no facilities, not even a microphone. And so, every night for four weeks, I had shouted the newscast from the anchor desk so that the assembled staff could hear it across the newsroom.

I was still shouting for the first month we were on the air. There was no rehearsal for that first newscast. The last piece of equipment we needed to get the signal out of the building came on stream thirty seconds before we went to air. The studio director gave me a miscue, and by the time the opening theme had finished, I was halfway through the third and final headline. I stopped and started again. Everything that could go wrong did. We lost film, tape items broke up on the air, our line-up fell to pieces, and we skipped from items early in the newscast to late ones and back again. It was a terrible beginning, but Cunningham had planted the seeds, and, in time, they grew. And even at the worst of times, it was never as bad as the CBC, because everyone cared, and everyone was trying.

Even our first director tried, although at times it was without much success. When things went wrong in the control room, he went into what one awed bystander described as a catatonic state. As a result, I would find myself sitting there on camera, with my face hanging out, not knowing what to do next. On one occasion, a classic of sorts, I was reduced to saying:

"All right, Mr. Director, I have read pages ten, seven, five, and fourteen. What would you like me to read next?"

I said it on the air. There was no other way, and the newscast's technical producer "logged" me for using a live on-air microphone as a control-room intercom.

I died and we died, night after night, but we got better. A measurable audience began to understand what it was we were trying to do, and slowly it grew.

Walter Cronkite is perhaps the best-known anchorman that television has yet produced. He is known far beyond the boundaries of the United States. As a matter of fact, he is so much a standard of the profession that in far-off Sweden, separated from the CBS viewing area by an ocean and a language, anchormen are known as "Cronkiters."

Cronkite is also the managing editor of CBS News, and it is not an empty label. He is involved in the CBS assigning process, that is, coming up with story ideas and plotting the disposition of the troops. He intervenes in the editing process, in the structuring of stories, and in the cutting of processed film. He is also involved in the preparation of the newscast itself. That is, he approves the line-up, the order of the stories appearing in the newscast; and he is also the chief writer, which means that he writes as much of his own material as possible, and carefully edits the rest. Cronkite may not exercise all the facets of his authority each day. It is a very heavy burden. But when he takes a newscast to air, he is in a position to be satisfied that it is the best CBS has been able to do that day. He believes what he is saying and what the CBS correspondents are saying. He feels the news, because he makes himself a part of it. He agonizes over the news, its emphasis, its accuracy. He is touched by it, and he conveys a sense of its drama. I am convinced that this involvement is what gives Cronkite credibility, the quality which the polls say make him one of the most influential men in America today.

I think that what has always disturbed me most about the CBC News, on the other hand, is that the man who reads "The National" appears to be detached and aloof. And I don't mean by that that he has an appearance of editorial impartiality, although he does convey that too. I mean that his style betrays a lack of involvement in the gathering, writing, and structuring of what he is saying.

There are, as I have mentioned, very good reasons for the detachment of a Knowlton Nash. The agreement between the Canadian Broadcasting Corporation and the Canadian Wire Service Guild, Local 213 of the American Newspaper Guild (AFL-CIO, CLC) read as follows, at least while I was at the CBC:

"The Corporation agrees that in programs produced by the CBC News Service the gathering, writing and editing of news, and associated duties, and the scripting of film and associated duties, shall be assigned only to employees within the bargaining unit."

At the same time, the agreement between the CBC and the Association of Radio and Television Employees of Canada (CUPE, CLC), the announcers' union, contained this jurisdictional guarantee:

"The following shall be performed exclusively by announcers: Reading of all newscasts and news flashes prepared by the News Service..."

Those two contractual passages constitute the irresistible force and the immovable object that have defied successive attempts by waves of executive producers and chief news editors to put the CBC's national newscasts in the hands of a working newsman. In public, at least, the corporation continues to fudge the issue.

When Knowlton Nash, then fifty years old, according to the newspapers was appointed to read "The National" in October of 1978, it was also announced that he would act as the news service's chief correspondent.

"I won't be writing," Nash told the press. "But what I'll be doing as chief correspondent is having some input into what we're doing on 'The National.' It's a team effort.''

CBS News is a team effort too, but the whole newscast bears Cronkite's imprimatur in a way that Nash will never be able to duplicate on ''The National,'' unless CBC management finally decides to force one of the two unions to drop the offending clause in its contract. ARTEC is easily the best bet. But until the challenge is met and beaten, Nash won't be an anchorman. He will continue to be a newsreader—a ''news actor,'' if you like—with superior qualifications.

Bill Cunningham hasn't missed the sweet justice of the bind in which Nash now finds himself. He has never forgiven Nash for his failure to push the '66 manifesto when he became the head of TV information programs, particularly in what it said about anchormen:

''Nash, as news director, along with Denis Harvey, when he was there, defended the status quo on the basis the public doesn't know the difference. Now Nash is saying you need a newsman to read the news. Why didn't he do something about it while he was in charge?''

The only time, in my own CBC experience, that Nash revealed any desire to make ''The National's'' host more than a mere reader was in 1969, when, in circumstances I have already described, he was trying to convince Warren Davis that, in John Nance Garner's words, the job was worth more than ''a bucket of warm spit.'' Davis wasn't persuaded for long. Ten years later, in an interview with TV Guide, he was still seething:

''The triviality of that job,'' he said, ''is indescribable. Before me, the Corporation decided they wanted a Cronkite, a hot-shot, so they found Stanley Burke, who was a hell of a reporter. He lasted a couple of years, before he got bored and left. When I came along, it was open warfare between newsmen and announcers. The news has never been read at the CBC by anyone who had anything to do with preparing it.

''The idea of a chief correspondent is simply window dressing. It doesn't exist. I think 'The National' is the best 'front page' in Canada, but it's never been read better than by Earl Cameron, who was an announcer. With Knowlton Nash, they're just building the sizzle. Nash must think the money and the fame are worth it, but the fame and a dime will buy you a phone call."

That's not quite fair, perhaps, to Nash, who has an opportunity to restore his soul as a working journalist on "Newsmagazine" and various news specials, including elections and conventions. The crippling union regulations apply only to newscasts. On specials, as Nash puts it, "you have to know what you're talking about."

But you still don't have to know what you're talking about on "The National," apparently. When Nash is on assignment, or vacation, he is replaced by announcers, often by George McLean, who has thirsted to do "The National" full time for years. His star now seems to be in the ascendancy again, although there was a period when Joe Schlesinger headed News and McLean was not even allowed to substitute on "The National." Schlesinger claimed that McLean never moved his upper lip.

I think Davis was right when he said that the CBC news was never read better than by Earl Cameron. For his time, Cameron was perfect. But Cameron, because he was an announcer and not a newsman, bore the seeds of his own destruction.

In those days, CBC announcers were allowed to do commercials. It was one of the perks of the job. An announcer's pay envelope was thin at that time, but by picking up some extra money doing commercials, he could aspire to a pretty decent living. Earl Cameron, because he was a good announcer, and because he was also the host of the national newscast, was something of a prize for advertisers. I remember two Cameron commercials in particular, one for toothpaste, the other for an automobile.

When Cunningham took over as executive producer, he argued successfully that this just wouldn't do. Having "The National's" newsreader flogging cars and toothpaste was not only damaging to Cameron's credibility, but to that of the news service. And so Cameron was forced to give up his lucrative commercial accounts. What was grossly unfair about all of this was the timing.

The CBC and Cunningham changed the rules, as far as Cameron was concerned, in mid-stream. And when, a few months later, Cunningham dropped Cameron and hired Stanley Burke, in pursuit of the impossible dream, Cameron felt he had been badly used. He had been.

Like most Canadians, I admired Cameron on the air, and with hundreds and thousands of others, waited nightly for that sparing and wonderful smile at the end of the newscast. But I had a deep personal affection for him too after a Press Gallery dinner in the spring of 1965, when speculation about his getting the chop first got into the papers.

The Gallery's annual dinner, to which reporters invite their bosses and the politicians, is always very much off the record. It is an evening of fun and serious drinking, and the Gallery members neglect their duties for weeks in advance as they work up skits and bawdy political songs for the big evening. Earl Cameron was invited to attend that year as a participant.

One of the skits called for an on-stage television set, and a body to read the national news. The TV set was a large, empty box, painted to look like the real thing, with a screen-shaped opening in place of a picture tube. Cameron was smuggled into the box before the skit began. At the appropriate moment, suddenly there he was, live and in person, his head and shoulders framed by that silly box, reading what was supposed to be the national news. It was tremendously effective and the crowd, feeling no pain, roared its approval. The last item in the fake newscast, for which Cameron did an appropriate double-take when he came across his own name, was a CBC announcement to the effect that he was being released as the reader of "The National." Although the punchline turned out to be prophetic, and Earl could not have been unaware of the movement to get rid of him, he entered into the spirit of the thing without reservation, and his wry good sportsmanship brought down the roof.

I got a nice note from Earl from his home in Lefroy, Ontario, early in 1976, shortly after they'd cancelled "Viewpoint" at the CBC, the vehicle I had used to get him back into late-night television. He enclosed a copy of the memo I'd written to John Rae, the chief announcer, asking that Earl be approached for the "Viewpoint" job. He had come across the memo while cleaning out his desk, and he was grateful for the things I'd said about him in that pitch for his services.

"Now that 'Viewpoint' has bit the dust," Earl wrote, "I guess that's it for TV for yours truly. I have enjoyed doing the show – so thanks again for your kind words. Keep up your good work on the tube – and take care."

I know what he means about taking care. Earl Cameron was and is a very classy guy.

Harvey Kirck, who has been hosting CTV's national newscast since December 1963, is a real anchorman, in the American sense of the word, but he falls short of the Cronkite prototype. He doesn't put in the kind of hours that Cronkite does, and his involvement isn't as complete. He noted in a recent magazine article that he gets to the office about 4:00 P.M. usually for an editorial production meeting.

"That's when we find out what we have going that day and what we're going to do with it," he says. He then breaks for dinner and comes back about 7:00 P.M. At that point, Kirck does become involved with the newscast in a meaningful way. He writes copy and edits video tape until about 9:45 P.M., when he goes for make-up. He gets a final script at 10:00, which he goes over, and may edit, and is in the studio for a rehearsal by 10:20. He goes on the air at 11:00, which means that CTV News doesn't reach the Maritimes until midnight, a factor in the ratings game. The CBC, incidentally, does a Maritime feed out of Toronto at 10:00 P.M. It really amounts to a rehearsal for the rest of the country, but it does mean that the Maritimes get a national newscast at the more civilized hour of 11:00 P.M. Atlantic time.

Harvey Kirck is quite clearly the dean of Canadian newscasters, not only because he has been at it longer than most of them in network television, but because his involvement in the newscast shows, and his professional background pays dividends in terms of believability. Don Cameron, CTV's vice-president of News, is on the record as a big fan of Kirck's.

"Harvey can do it all," Cameron says. "Report, write, read. He's a fully integrated part of the operation, not just a performer."

Harvey should frame that quote, because in the jungle of network television, there may come a time when he'll need it. I think that although Kirck is the closest thing we have to a Canadian

Cronkite, he's wrong in many of his judgements about news in general and television news in particular. In an article for *Weekend Magazine*, on December 16, 1978, Kirck wrote:

"It's ridiculous to criticize TV for being too shallow. Television can't tell you all – it was designed to highlight events. Pomp and pageantry, the investiture of a Pope or coronation of a King or Queen – TV covers those things better than any other medium. We are not really in competition with the newspapers. People still have to read the papers to be well-informed."

He's right in thinking that TV news will never take the place of the newspapers. But it seems to me that to dismiss television as a picture medium, fit only for colourful events, is curiously dated, with some validity perhaps thirty years ago, when Edward R. Murrow, still in radio, held that view. But to cling to it today, when we're just beginning to learn how to use television for news, is to quit in the middle of the game.

What I like best about Harvey Kirck is his longevity. Any damned fool can read a newscast for a week or two. But to get up off the canvas night after night, shake your head and do it again, whether you're sick, hung-over, or just plain bored, month after month, year after year – that's what separates the men from the boys.

I don't know what Harvey Kirck and Lloyd Robertson get paid. I haven't asked them. But if they do make the reported $100,000 a year, or close to it, they're worth every nickel.

When CTV's Tom Gould, then the vice-president, first began dickering with the CBC's Robertson, the Toronto press was full of rumours that Harvey was going to be dumped. Like much of the stuff printed in the Toronto entertainment pages about the industry, that rumour turned out to be untrue.

At that point, certainly, CTV would have been crazy to fire Kirck. By hanging onto him and adding Lloyd Robertson to the line-up, the network was able to fence off its existing ratings, and send Lloyd out on a raid for former CBC viewers. And it worked, at least to a degree. CTV's ratings soon began to move. There were people in the business who felt it wouldn't, that the Kirck faction, which liked his tough, truck-driver delivery, would be put off by pretty-boy Robertson, and that the Robertson faction, which preferred nice news, would find Kirck too abrasive for their delicate palates.

The critics were probably right in sheer program terms. The CTV format has never managed to establish the need for two anchormen. There is no natural division of labour. The most successful duo to ever grace network news, Chet Huntley and David Brinkley, worked together with a geographic and stylistic rationale. Huntley did it from New York, and Brinkley did the Washington news. Huntley was solid, kindly, reassuring. Brinkley was waspish, wry, and cutting.

But Kirck and Robertson sit knee-to-knee in a badly designed set which emphasizes Harvey's bulk and Lloyd's prim diminutiveness. There is a story told about the two men's chairs, which may well be apocryphal, but which is certainly in keeping with what I know of Harvey.

Someone around the new set during the dry runs made a move to lower Harvey's chair so that he and Lloyd would appear to be nearer the same height. Quietly but firmly, Harvey is supposed to have told this well-meaning leveller that if he touched the Kirck chair he was dead.

Otherwise, relations between the two have been reasonably good. I have it on solid authority that Lloyd refused to consider coming to CTV unless the network paid Harvey the same considerable sum it was prepared to pay him. It was not only a humanitarian move on Lloyd's part. It is probably the only reason the relationship still works.

In the end, Lloyd's defection from the CBC probably did the corporation some good. Although the CBC's newsreaders had been crippled by the two union contracts for years, the people who wrote about television, at least in Toronto, never seemed to have understood. Lloyd's departure at least forced that long-standing idiocy into the open. Scott Young, writing in the *Globe,* isolated part of the problem.

"The interference of the Canadian Wire Service Guild with what Lloyd Robertson has a perfect right to think was his natural function − to go out and do some reporting from time to time −

was intolerable, and nobody with guts would take it for long. After a certain stage, money means little or nothing, but career fulfilment means more and more as a person gets older.''

Dennis Braithwaite, commenting on Peter Kent's appointment in the *Star*, got closer to the real issue:

''Yet though Peter Kent's credentials as a journalist are exemplary, he will not be writing the stuff he reads on 'The National.' Adhering to the dictate it laid down for his predecessors, the Canadian Wire Services Guild, a subsidiary of the American Newspaper Guild (AFL-CIO, CLC) will not permit Kent to type a single line of what he reads.

''Thus we have the anomaly of Lloyd Robertson, an announcer, leaving the CBC in part to escape the union's prohibition against free speech, being replaced by a bona fide newsman to whom the same restriction will apply.

''Why does the CBC tolerate union interference with its right to run its news department as it sees fit? Because it happens to suit the corporation's purpose not to have a journalist writing the news as well as reading it. A gelded reader satisfactorily fulfils the CBC's requirement of purity in news.''

As usual, Braithwaite was only partly right. The real reason that CBC management doesn't settle the newsman/anchorman question once and for all is that it doesn't dare run the risk of a major strike by one of the two unions as its contract expires. If the CBC had convictions, and matching guts, it would have settled the whole business years ago.

Lloyd Robertson, off the screen, is pretty well the same Lloyd Robertson who co-hosts CTV's national newscast. He is not only the smoothest newsreader in the country, he is also a devoted husband and family man and a pillar of the church. A lot of news has rubbed off on him in the past few years, but he is not in Kirck's league as a writer or a journalist.

I first met Lloyd in 1968, when he was a back-up reader to Stanley Burke. Our relationship was a good one from the beginning. When I was his boss, I used to chaff Lloyd about his hair. He was always perfectly groomed, every hair in place, and I used to tell him: ''For God's sake, Lloyd, muss it up a little. You don't look real.''

Years later, when I first began reading Global News, I got a letter from a woman who didn't think much of me or the newscast. But she reserved her most scathing comments for the unnatural perfection of my grooming. "For God's sake," she wrote me. "Muss up your hair." I replied as best I could and sent a copy of the correspondence to Lloyd. It was only fair.

Although Lloyd was on the announce staff at the CBC, he was an early convert to the reporter/announcer concept. Sometime before Warren Davis threw in the sponge, and before Lloyd was annointed by the Kremlin, I think I levelled with him about why he wasn't exactly my ideal. I treated him to my standard harangue about why a newscast should be hosted and written by someone deeply involved in its preparation.

As a matter of fact, I offered to make Lloyd an editor-reporter if he would give up his announcer's salary and join the news service as a member of the Guild. For some reason or other, I didn't feel I could sweeten the offer with an overscale contract, so Lloyd, as a breadwinner, refused. It would have cost him a good deal of money – somewhere between $5,000 and $10,000 a year – and that, at the time, was a sacrifice he didn't feel he could make.

Lloyd has picked up considerable news savvy almost by osmosis. But he continues to believe that the anchorman-journalist mystique is overworked. As he told Barbara Byers of *Broadcaster* magazine in April 1977:

"If you've worked in news, if you've read it, gathered it and reported it for twenty-five years, that's as much experience as someone coming in with five years, newspaper experience."

It's no secret that for a time when he first went to CTV, Lloyd was homesick for the CBC. It was plastered all over the front pages of the *Globe and Mail* one Saturday morning in December 1976, just a couple of months after he'd switched networks. The fact that Lloyd had been talking to the mother corporation again had been deliberately leaked to the *Globe* by someone at CBC. If that didn't convince Robertson to stay where he was, CTV president Murray Chercover's angry reminder that he had a binding contract certainly did.

The *Globe* struck a low blow, in my view, by pumping Robertson's wife Nancy about the story. Inexperienced as most people are about dealing with reporters, she said a great deal more than she should have. She must have felt sick when she read the *Globe* that morning and saw what her own innocent comments looked like in print:

"After twenty-two years," she said, according to the *Globe,* "he still hasn't lost his love for the CBC. The CTV is more of a commercial organization."

Just how commercial became evident when Chercover spoke to the *Globe,* "angrily," it was reported, the same evening. He said that the possibility of Robertson leaving the CTV simply didn't exist.

"He finds this place – as most journalists do – a very desirable place to work."

According to the newspaper, Chercover refused to answer "rhetorical or hypothetical questions," and said he would not discuss any aspect of Robertson's commitment to CTV.

"The general practice is a contract – it binds both parties to each other and both parties are expected, if out of nothing else but honour, to live up to their part of the bargain. . . Don't you know what a contract is? Look it up in the dictionary!"

I won't dwell on Chercover or CTV here. Suffice it to say that a considerable number of journalists have found CTV an undesirable place to work, and that no contract is forever. By an odd sort of coincidence, my own contract with CTV several months later was based on Robertson's. CTV was in breach of my contract as far as I was concerned. And so I quit.

But it wasn't to go to the CBC. Of that I had long since been cured. When Robertson first went to CTV in the fall of 1976, my name kept cropping up in the TV columns as a possible replacement. But I was never really in the running. Knowlton Nash and other CBC executives spoke to the newspapers about the possibility of my replacing Robertson, but not once in the period between Robertson's departure and Kent's appointment did anyone from the CBC so much as contact me. I would have been surprised if they had. I already had a job, of course, and the CBC didn't have one to offer.

Despite his youth, at thirty-three, Peter Kent was the logical choice. The year before, he had won the ACTRA news award for his daring reporting on the finale of the Cambodian struggle, the fall of Phnom Penh. He was and is a first-class journalist, with a rare combination of guts and polish.

The only thing Kent didn't have was a track record for staying put. In the space of only a few months, he had jumped from CTV's London bureau to the ranks of the unemployed, joined the fledgling Global news service as a reporter, quit Global to go sailing on Georgian Bay, and finally settled at the CBC. Knowing Kent and his taste for action (he is the kind of guy, who, while he was at Global, had to try a parachute jump simply because he had never jumped before), most of us didn't give him a year before he became bored to tears. For someone like Kent, sitting behind a desk reading someone else's copy was bound to be unappealing, and eventually, unbearable.

At Global and CTV, we rubbed our hands in anticipation. When the opposition keeps changing faces, it's good for business. In fact, Kent lasted two years. And after delivering a broadside to CBC management for knuckling under to unreasonable requests for air-time by the Prime Minister's office – a breach of corporate etiquette that would have cost him his job anywhere but at the CBC – he lunged off happily to Nairobi, to open the CBC's first African bureau. Kent wasn't ordered to Nairobi in disgrace, as the general public seemed to think. Both he and news management saw it as a kind of pay-off for sticking out "The National" for two tough years.

After little more than a year in Nairobi, Kent finally completed the quitting process. He resigned from the CBC to go to NBC in January 1980. The CBC's chief news editor, Cliff Lonsdale, remarked rather plaintively that Kent was one of the network's best correspondents, and it was inevitable that he would be sought after by one of the American networks.

Shortly after Kent quit "The National," in the fall of 1978, Bill Cunningham got a hot tip from someone in the CBC that Knowlton Nash was going to be the next newsreader. In my role as a newsman, I phoned Nash at home, and put the question to him straight. It was after all, a good story.

"Confirm or deny that you will be replacing Peter Kent as ''The National's'' newsreader,'' I told him.

"Nothing's happening on that one,'' Knowlton said, ''and there probably won't be any decision on it for a week or so anyway.''

He went on to say that there were a lot of names on the list, Trueman's included, and, he added, ''maybe mine, too.'' A few weeks later it was official. Nash was the new reader.

If the other people on the CBC's ''list'' were no closer to being actual candidates than I was, then the list might just as well have been compiled from a casual reading of the trade journals. Once again, no one from the CBC had so much as telephoned. I wouldn't have been interested, of course, even if I had been willing to leave Global. But I would have liked being asked. It would have given me considerable satisfaction to have refused, and once again explain why.

CHAPTER FIVE

The Mouth
and His Money

Even when an anchorman rolls up his sleeves and plunges into the writing and preparation of a newscast, it can be a soul-destroying business. For one thing, he is desk-bound. He builds the frames for other people's masterpieces. I don't hear the firebells now, the way I used to when I first became an anchorman, perhaps because I'm getting older. But there are times when I think that if I can't get out of the office with a good camera crew, I'll explode. One of the reasons I left the CBC, the first time, was that I realized I would much rather do things myself than spend my life telling other people how to do them.

A good anchorman must not only be a good journalist. He must have stamina and stability. He must not only have the credentials to do the job for a week. He must have the strength and evenness of disposition to do it for years. To some extent, this is a new problem in Canada. In the past, when the news host was only a reader, it wasn't as critical. He had already accepted the fact that as an announcer, his job was to read, on a daily basis, with only the annual vacation as a break in the routine. But even then, there was strain, the strain of performance.

There was a period at the CBC when Lloyd Robertson was not only hosting "The National," but was reading the Toronto regional news. He did it successfully for a time, but I know it was a strain.

Anyone who is dead calm, unemotional when he reads, may be in trouble. In my experience, you had better be on the edge of your seat. And so two newscasts is a bit like a hockey player "getting up'' for two games on the same day; or like an actor having to do an afternoon and evening performance of different plays.

But now that almost everyone except the CBC has accepted the dictum that an anchorman also has to work at the substance of the newscast, the question of stamina and emotional balance has become much more pressing. There is no easy way to do a professional television newscast, despite a suggestion I read a few years ago in a newspaper profile of Don Jameison, then the minister for External Affairs, by an American correspondent at the United Nations. The admiring newspaper man noted that Jameison had had ten years as a highly successful politician since ''the days in St. John's when he went before live TV cameras and did half-hour news shows without script and without 'idiot cards', extemporizing from notes.''

If the description of Jameison's modus operandi is accurate, it must have been some newscast. For one thing, if he really just chatted to his viewers without a script, the newscast could not have carried very much film. The director must have a script to know when to roll film, or the man reading the news is likely to be cut off in mid-sentence. Either that or he has to sit there, blankly, with nothing to say, until the film finally appears. In most newsrooms, the director must have precisely three seconds' warning if the film is to appear when the host stops speaking. There is only one way to make a newscast look easy, and that is to prepare it carefully, word by word, second by second, right down to the closing credits.

Shortly after Global went on the air, I found myself doing two newscasts a day, a grind that was to last for more than three years. My day began long before we got down to actual script. I had no secretarial or research assistance from Global, which meant that my wife and I had to handle all the phone calls and all the mail. It meant that if I didn't get an idea early for a closing comment – what amounted to a daily broadcast column – I was going to be a one-armed paperhanger later in the day. From the beginning, I was feeding stuff into the assignment desk – story ideas and how they should be developed – giving the vice-president a sounding board on personnel and strategy, acting as the chief news writer and script editor, and functioning as a one-man public relations bureau for the struggling news service, and to some extent the network. I spent a lot of time in high-school auditoriums and at service club lunches.

The only thing that saved me, I am convinced, is that I am a jogger. If I hadn't been in reasonably good physical condition, I'd have dropped in my tracks at the end of the first season. As it was, I was beyond the point of physical exhaustion when I finally threw in the sponge, and of course I wasn't alone. We'd all been doing the work of two people.

When Michael Maclear called from CTV, I was ready. He had been appointed to develop a new concept in public affairs programming, to be known perhaps as "The Reporters." He wanted to know if I would be interested in a job as the main host. The prospect of two shows a week (Thursday and Sunday) instead of ten, and the chance to travel and report in the days intervening, was enormously appealing.

Since my three-year contract with Global had expired some months previously, and I was operating on the basis of a personal undertaking to Cunningham, I agreed to meet him. Soon, I was talking not only to Maclear, but to the news vice-president of the network, my old boss and employee, Don Cameron. At that stage, I told them to get serious. Either make me an offer I couldn't refuse, or forget it. They did, and without informing Cunningham, I took it.

Cunningham was hurt and angry. He thought he had my word, and by then I was too punchy to know whether he did or didn't. Despite the fact that I had made it clear to him that two newscasts were killing me, he was taken completely by surprise, and he said some things in the heat of the moment that were difficult to forgive.

Between my resignation and the actual date of my departure (I had foolishly given them two months' notice so that Global would have ample time to line up a replacement), I was subjected to a Cunningham blitz. On one occasion, he trapped me on a plane to Winnipeg, and subjected me to his own considerable charm, and all the arguments he knew would appeal to me, for more than an hour.

Alan Slaight, still the president of Global at that point, offered me a financial deal which in its simplest terms meant that I could have gone off to write books or make documentaries in about five years. When Slaight lost Global and the new president, Paul Morton, took over, he reaffirmed the offer. Even then, I was beginning to feel I had made a terrible mistake, but I felt that I had to honour my word to CTV, and when I finally went, my chief emotion was relief. At last I was out from under the full weight of Cunningham's silent, and not-so-silent reproach.

"CTV Reports," as the network finally decreed the new program would be known, had an embarrassment of riches: budget, producers, film crews, support staff, hosts and ideas. From a big fish in a small pond, I had become a minnow in an ocean. Quite apart from the damage to my ego, there was the damage to my confidence. And aside from what I like to think was one atypical moment at an early staff meeting, when I informed a slightly incredulous audience that I had a rare gift for getting through the box and reaching viewers, I was hesitant and miserable.

The set was cold and hollow and I felt lost in it. Although I shot four stories in a trip around the world the summer before we went on the air, only one of them had been broadcast, in fragments, when I quit the network. I was involved in other stories, in a peripheral way for the most part. Often, I found myself being dropped into other people's stories in mid-shoot, to do a fast piece to camera in some appropriate location, and then be whisked away to be parachuted into something else. It was the antithesis of what I had expected, and whatever it was, it wasn't my idea of journalism.

Maclear, who must be one of the best correspondents anywhere, proved to be one of the worst executive producers. He fought endless battles that he couldn't win against the brass on the next floor, and he was unable to delegate authority. One of the reasons he hired me, he had said during the negotiations, was that I could write a script. But often when I had finished one, I was reduced to defending it, sentence by sentence, as Maclear sought to impose his very considerable will. Perhaps I'd been my own boss too long.

The situation with Maclear was complicated by the fact that two of his main front-line producers were news traditionalists, who would have been, and as a matter of fact had been, adornments to network newsrooms, but whose judgements, in my view, tended to be an anathema to the more analytical structure and approach of a weekly public affairs program.

CTV, perhaps leery of the fact that my unlovely face was unknown nationally, apparently urged Maclear not to let his own face disappear from view. The end result was a horrendous traffic jam at the make-up room. We had hosts to burn: me, Bruce Phillips, CTV's Ottawa bureau chief; Barbara Amiel, of *Maclean's* magazine; Bill Stevenson, the author and freelance producer; André Payette, now Joe Clark's press secretary, and then one of the best-known television personalities in Quebec; and Maclear. It made it difficult for any of us to make any kind of an impression on the program or the viewers.

The ratings of our much-ballyhooed program sank quickly, and Don Cameron finally stepped in to plug the leaks. He fired Maclear as executive producer of the "CTV Reports" package, and made him host and producer of the half-hour Wednesday-night segment. Amiel, Phillips, and I were made the hosts of the Sunday-night hour.

As far as I was concerned, things went from bad to worse. I was now completely at the mercy of the two news producers, and had less chance than ever to get my imprint on anything. The last straw came in November, when I returned to Toronto after covering the Israeli reaction to that first historic Sadat visit.

Les Rose, my field producer, and I cut what we felt was a sensitive and moving package on the Israelis' mingled hope and disbelief. The producer who screened it was not moved. He could hardly conceal his boredom. Although it was already at ten or eleven minutes – the minimum length we felt we needed to develop the mood – he wanted it cut still further. He said it was the kind of thing we should have run a week earlier. I refused to cut it, and I finally put it to him this way:

"You cut it, as you see fit, and then call me. I'll screen it, and if I can live with your version, I'll take it to air. If I can't, get yourself another boy."

It was finally broadcast the way Les and I wanted it, but for me, already dispirited, it had been one battle too many. At the right moment, I heard that Cunningham, who had practically been stopping strangers on the street to tell them what a schmuck I was, had a change of heart. My old job, or rather half my old job, might be available at Global News. That, and the fact that I felt I had to do something quickly to maintain professional credibility, decided me.

I sat down and wrote a long memo to Cameron, in which I listed my grievances and accused CTV of breaching the contract. It was fortunate that I had insisted on certain additions to the Robertson contract that we'd used as a model.

Among them was a clause in which CTV agreed that I should not be required to do anything which would bring me into "disrepute," and another in which both parties to the contract agreed that they would do nothing which would "encroach on the other's standards of journalistic integrity."

As host of "CTV Reports," I had been obliged to read scripts which I couldn't completely believe in because I hadn't researched the stories or written the scripts myself; I had been obliged to lend my face and voice to projects with which I didn't agree; and if I wasn't actually in "disrepute" as a result of the program's mismanagement, I certainly wasn't covered with roses. In the memo, I warned Cameron that I would start job-hunting immediately. I called Bill Cunningham and asked him to have lunch. For the first time, I apologized to him for quitting without giving him a chance to negotiate, and I admitted that I had been wrong. After that, we buried the hatchet rather quickly. The *Toronto Sun*'s television critic, Bob Blackburn, telephoned me at home when my reappointment was announced, and in between my "no comments," accused me of jumping from one network to another to build up the size of my contract. The truth of the matter was that I lost money on both moves. I had gone to CTV for less than Global was offering me to stay. And I had gone back to Global for less than I had been making at CTV.

But my chief concern at that point was not money. It was how Rae Corelli would take the return of the prodigal. Cunningham had begun dickering with Corelli, then the *Toronto Star*'s legal correspondent, some months before I left Global. An indication that Corelli would do one of the two newscasts, after Global had a chance to break him in, had been one of the carrots dangled before me as I was trying to get out the door.

When I quit, Cunningham, with unerring instinct, advanced the timetable. He hired Corelli immediately. Corelli went on the air the Labour Day of the summer I left and he made anchoring look easy. I watched the first newscast, and I couldn't believe it. Corelli looked and sounded as if he'd been doing it for years.

When Cunningham rehired me, Corelli not only made it easy for me, but welcomed me with open arms. It wasn't entirely selfless, of course. The charm of two newscasts a day was already beginning to pall, and without very much prompting he confessed he had no idea how I had been able to do it for three years.

After another year, Corelli found that the frustration of even one newscast a day was too much to take. He had waged an unending battle to raise Global's journalistic practices to a level he could be comfortable with. To his credit, "the Judge" has never been easy to satisfy journalistically, and the difference between the editorial practice of a Metropolitan daily and a TV newsroom was one he hadn't completely understood or forgiven. So he decided to take on the Saturday newscast, absorb a cut in salary, and use the extra time to write a book.

A print newsman faces enormous personal problems when he turns his talents to TV. Corelli always resented what he called "the star crap," and when our promotion people asked us to pose for billboard photos, or do a walkthrough for promotional spots, he did it glowering. It was always a problem getting a picture of the Judge in which he didn't look murderous. Corelli never had any problem with ego, and like a lot of us, found that being recognized on the street was an advantage he didn't need.

It is one of the anomalies of the business that when an on-air personality begins to be successful, he may find himself resenting its fruits, that is, recognition. The only way I can cope with my own feelings about this, controlling the impulse to use four-letter greetings on people who regard me as public property, is to remind myself that if I were not recognized, I would be quickly out of work. And sometimes, in a restaurant, it will get me a better table.

I first became personally aware of the awful power of the tube when I was working for the *Toronto Star* during the '65 election campaign. The man who brought it home to me was Norman DePoe, then at the height of his career, and one of the best-known faces on Canadian television. He was really the Ottawa anchorman for CBC News. The CBC was running a promotional campaign at the time, which they called ''Starburst '65.'' At the height of the campaign, we kept running into billboards on which the CBC's most familiar faces were framed by exploding stars. One of the faces, of course, was Norman's, and although he had grace enough to be chagrined by it, it must have been an enormous fillip to his already considerable ego.

About that time, Ralph Allen, then the editor of the *Toronto Star,* asked me to do a colour piece on ''old Norman.'' The tone of the profile was set in the lead, where I think I compared DePoe's rakish presence on Earl Cameron's austere nightly newscast to a riverboat gambler at a PTA meeting.

In it, I related the story of a night in that '65 election campaign (I think we were with Diefenbaker at the time), when a group of newsmen were drinking and singing in somebody's room at the old CPR hotel in Winnipeg. It was the middle of the night, and, not unexpectedly, there came a peremptory knock at the door.

DePoe, still rasping a chorus, went to the door singing. He pulled it open a crack, saw that it was a uniformed CPR policeman, then turned his back on him and finished the song. When there was quiet, the policeman opened his mouth to speak. ''Go away,'' said Norman, and closed the door in the policeman's face. Oddly enough, the policeman stayed away, and we went on with our singing. It was an impressive demonstration of the power of ''Starburst '65.'' If anyone else had closed the door in the policeman's face we would probably have done the rest of our singing in the clink.

Years later at the CBC, when I was having a row with Norman over something or other, he sought to use his undoubted audience appeal to bring me to his way of thinking.

He had been covering some Prime Minister or other on a tour of western Canada and as sometimes happened many of the people in the crowd had been more interested in Norman than in the Canadian leader. Thinking it might help in his ongoing duel with me, Norman had his cameramen shoot a hundred feet of film of the crowd besieging him for his autograph.

Back in Toronto, he slammed the processed roll on my desk with an air of triumph, and suggested that I should treat him with respect. I calmed him down finally by persuading him that whatever I proposed was because I was his biggest fan and that I wanted his autograph too.

DePoe was a public figure not only because he was good at what he did, but because he got so much air-time. And he continued to get the air-time not only because he was a good reporter, but because he wore well.

It is a quality which is vital for anchormen who intrude nightly into the inner sanctums of a nation's viewers. Those who are instantly acceptable, sometimes don't last well. Familiarity sometimes breeds contempt. Others come on more slowly, growing in the job and growing on the viewers. Walter Cronkite set no audience records early in his anchoring career. He improved with age, like good whisky or old cheddar. The ones who last tend to be an acquired taste. They have dimension and sharp edges. They irritate and amuse.

That is one reason why networks change anchormen so infrequently. They don't want to risk upsetting the acquired taste of their viewers. A news habit is difficult to induce. That gives the network anchorman a bigger and bigger lever as time goes on. And that is why in the end, a good one can command the earth.

In the United States, salaries have gone berserk. It makes the row over the money paid to Kirck, Robertson and Nash seem somewhat foolish. Whatever those three earn, it is safe to say that no network anchorman in this country at the moment makes much more than $100,000 a year, and that, in the United States, $100,000 is the going minimum not for network anchormen, but the anchormen at large individual stations.

When Barbara Walters went to ABC, and became the first news-caster to earn $1,000,000 in a single year, the American dam had burst. Neither the networks nor their expensive creations are very anxious to discuss salaries, but one way or another, through a combination of leaks and guesstimates, figures have found their way into print.

And it quickly emerged that from the network's point of view, Barbara Walters' million dollars need only be the beginning. As one lawyer agent remarked briskly:

"It would have been worth a million dollars to ABC just to send Barbara to sit on a beach in the south of France. At least they would have eliminated her from NBC."

Ms. Walters was hardly underpaid as the co-host of NBC's "Today" show. The guessing was that NBC paid her $700,000 a year for that job, plus a number of perks, which included a chauffeured limousine to take her to and from work.

And all she had to do for ABC, without calculating what her vanishing from NBC was worth, to repay their annual cash outlay in full, was to raise ABC's share of the audience watching network news by a single percentage point. That single point would have raised ABC's news revenues by $1,000,000 a year. Unfortunately, she couldn't do it immediately. After a month and a half, ABC's ratings had improved only slightly, and despite Ms. Walters, the newscast was still running third.

As long ago as 1975, Walter Cronkite was reputed to be making $750,000 a year. But I'm dubious about that figure, if only be-cause of the tenor of Cronkite's outrage when the Walters story broke. But if $750,000 was anywhere near the mark in 1975, it was probably close to Barbara Walters' million by 1980. In the same year, NBC's John Chancellor was reputed to be making $600,000. And the word was out that Harry Reasoner, later to become Walters' reluctant partner, was pulling down $400,000 at ABC.

Tom Snyder, as host of NBC's "Tomorrow" show, the an-chorman of NBC's Sunday night news, and the anchorman of NBC's local week-night newscasts in New York City, was supposed to be making $500,000 in 1975. But the only thing that is surprising about that is that he was still alive to collect a paycheque.

It isn't just the money that keeps a number of talented Canadians working for the American networks, but it must help. I don't know how many times Canadian broadcast executives have tried and failed to get ABC's Peter Jennings back to Canada.

Jennings went to ABC in 1964, at the height of the presidential election campaign, Johnson vs Goldwater, of that year. He'd started his television career in Canada and had done very well, but he knew he needed some international seasoning, and when the U.S. networks beckoned, Jennings was ready. Before long, he was anchoring the ABC network's evening newscast. It was a meteoric rise, and the CBC was moved to do a profile on his success.

On the evening that the CBC aired the program, Charles and Liz Jennings, Peter's parents, were attending an Ottawa party being given by "Tony" Lovink, then the Dutch Ambassador. Charles, who was one of the CBC's senior executives and one of the Canadian network's first announcers, was quite rightly proud of his son's incredible success. And so he and his wife disappeared upstairs to the ambassador's family sitting room when the program came on the air. But the anchor job didn't last. Peter just wasn't ready to take on Walter Cronkite and Huntley-Brinkley at the same time. So when ABC put him out as a foreign correspondent to see if they could put some wrinkles on that handsome face, Peter saw it as an opportunity.

Today, he has what must be the dream job of U.S. network television. He is the European anchorman for ABC News, based in London, with a Lear jet standing by and a mandate to cover anything on that side of the world that is worth his attention.

At least three times that I know of, serious attempts have been made to get him to come back to Canada. The CBC has tried a couple of times and I am pretty certain that Jennings headed Cunningham's first list for Global. I don't think that money – at least personal money, salary – has ever been the primary consideration in Jennings' decision not to return. It's just that once you've experienced the challenges and sophistication of the big leagues, it must be tough to go back to the sandlot again. Jennings has a lot of big league ball left in him.

Morley Safer, co-anchor and co-author of the stunning success that CBS has had with "60 Minutes," is also a Canadian. He started with the CBC in Toronto, but he built his American reputation on his courageous coverage of the Vietnam war, and I doubt that he can ever come home again. Again, it wouldn't be a question of salary, but of the kind of news gathering machine that he could be part of here.

Robert MacNeil, the New York anchorman for PBS's "MacNeil-Lehrer Report," is another expatriate. I knew him slightly at what was then Carleton College in Ottawa's Glebe district in the early fifties. The son of a former commissioner of the RCMP, MacNeil was helping to finance his way through college by doing station breaks and other "announce" duties at CBOT. MacNeil has had considerable success on several levels. He has been a correspondent for the American commercial networks, and has also become a well-known broadcast personality in Britain. He is at home personally and professionally on two continents and in three countries, and he is a studious, thoughtful, and penetrating reporter. We've come closer to getting MacNeil back to Canada, I think, than any of them. Cunningham had a good run at him when Global first went on the air, and negotiations were serious enough for protracted talks. And when I quit Global to go to CTV, Cunningham managed to land him as host for Global's "Lives" series. So at least Canada has had a piece of him again.

The only thing that would bring any of them back to Canada full time would be much higher Canadian standards and a greater opportunity for professional satisfaction than now exists north of the border. We make good information television programs in this country, but not consistently. We simply haven't got the money for consistency. And although, in my view, it is more satisfying to do merely acceptable programming on a shoe-string budget than it is to do merely acceptable programming on a large budget, it is no substitute for doing programming that you can be proud of without reservation. And no Canadian network, in terms of philosophy, running money, facilities, and professional back-up can hold a candle to the best of the British and American machines.

Some people feel that the days of the anchorman are numbered. Richard Wald, president of NBC News, in a speech he made to the National Association of Broadcasters at Chicago in April of 1976, peeked into the future.

"I think," said Wald, "that what we have always come to regard as anchormen will not work the way they work now. That is, our traditional sense of what a network anchorman is, in effect, is the all-wise, all-seeing mouth. That person who knows everything and will tell it to you too. That person never really existed, but because you now know the world to be as complicated as indeed it is, he can't exist in the popular fantasy. It may be that Walter Cronkite is the last of the great talkers."

What will replace the anchorman, Wald suggested, is wall-to-wall pictures, courtesy of the mini-cam and ENG, electronic news gathering. In Wald's less than convincing view of the future, a newscast will have no set, no anchorperson. Its set will be the world, its central figures the people who make the news. Frankly, I don't really believe it.

I think that one way or another, anchormen will always be needed. Someone to write and deliver the main points, to pull the news together, to put a human imprint on the whole package. Someone who has been involved in the process all day, all week, all year, who knows the circumstances under which a story was assigned and where it fits into the news fabric of that particular day.

Harry Boyle, the distinguished broadcaster and author who chaired the CRTC, has put his finger on one of the faults of television news in this country:

"It's bitsy and piecey," he told a reporter in 1978. "Confrontations and catastrophes. . . and it doesn't really contribute very much to understanding, or any thought process or analysis."

Anchormen who can fit the bits and pieces into the context of our rapidly changing times, and who can assign some significance to the confrontations and catastrophes, or drop them completely, won't be replaced by ENG or anything else, in this century.

As a matter of fact, it is now becoming clear that ENG is likely to enhance the anchorman's role by enabling him to do newscasts from the scene of the story. If that trend continues, watch grey-haired anchormen disappear. They're going to get younger and stronger. They'll have to.

CHAPTER SIX

The Backroom Boys

Despite its many charms, network news is a vicious, incestuous, all-consuming business. Most of the men who run television news operations work too hard, drink too much, and live too little. They tend to be totally involved with and absorbed by the news. What passes for private lives is also largely news. After work, they eat and talk, drink and scheme with the people they haven't been able to fit in during the day. Bill Cunningham's idea of a vacation is to go to a television industry conference in Mexico, spend a week with Robert MacNeil on his boat, and take a few more days in St. Andrew's, N.B., with his mother and other relations. That was what he planned in the summer of 1979, his first vacation of any significance in three years. What he actually did was to attend the conference in Mexico, and then fly back to the Toronto newsroom with baling wire and chewing gum, to help get it through the summer.

Needless to say, the kind of lives that network news people lead are not conducive to happy marriages. Six recent or current news executives I have picked at random have had at least fourteen marriages that I know of, plus at least two fairly solid "arrangements" that are at least as permanent as any of their short-lived nuptials. Reduced to its crudest terms, it means that on the average, they have gone through almost three wives apiece. And most of them are young enough that if they manage to survive the first heart attack, the statistics on their marriages may not yet be all in.

Happy marriages are possible in the TV news business, but it takes a strong sense of priorities, will-power, and something less than utter dedication to the news. Shop talk ends more newsroom marriages than the eternal triangle.

Bill Cunningham runs Global News with the conviction that any news chief who is not engaged in a constant screaming contest with the people who control the network's purse strings just isn't doing his job. To the layman and the network accountant alike, news is a hideously expensive business, and the owners and the network news chiefs must, because of the opposing nature of their responsibilities, spend many of their waking hours at each other's throats.

The commercial network's first job is to stay on the air and make money for its shareholders. The news executive's job is to cover the news, as completely as possible. There is never enough money for that, and there never will be. But news, particularly in Canada, can also be a smart investment, how smart the commercial networks show no sign of realizing.

When Bill Cunningham turned his back on the two biggest news machines, the CBC's and CTV's, it was a decision for quality instead of quantity, a target that has not always been realized.

Although still in his forties, Cunningham has spent more than twenty-five years in news, a career that has taken him back and forth across Canada and around the world many times. He was born in New Brunswick, of solid, old Maritime stock, went to high school and played hockey in what the chamber of commerce called "the Hub of the Maritimes," Moncton, N.B., and although I was growing up in nearby Sackville and Fredericton about the same time, we met for the first time in a bar years later in Tuscaloosa, Alabama. One of Bill's first jobs was as a bellhop in a Moncton hotel. The panache and the accoutrements of some of the salesmen he lugged Gladstones for made a lasting impression, and Cunningham has been inclined to go first class ever since. To this day, I think, he is happiest on the road.

He has never made one of those best-dressed lists, although he should have. One of his women friends, who knows something about fashion, says that Cunningham "dresses like a dream." He's inclined to tweeds and flannels, twill and good linen, and winter or summer, like many of our generation from the Maritimes, wears wool ties. He likes good leather, good rum, and has a passion for teak and brass, particularly in ships. He looks like a cross between Humphrey Bogart and Alan Ladd, a quality that did him no harm as a foreign correspondent. Cunningham is inclined to dismiss his own prowess as a correspondent, but as a former boss I can testify that, although it cost the earth to send him on a long swing, it always paid off. I can't remember a dull Cunningham story, although he must have done some. Everyone does.

He is one of the most persuasive talkers I know, a quality which has given me trouble for years. After I've talked to him, and I once again find myself agreeing to something I didn't want to do, I reflect on the ease with which he can con me.

He has a passion for quality, not just relating to production but in terms of people. He's inclined to gamble on them, hope that the quality he detects will emerge in time so that everyone can see it. When he is right about someone, it can often be demonstrated that he was right about them long before anyone else was. But when he does make a wrong call, it's really wrong, and he is generally the last to admit it.

Cunningham is the kind of administrator who works out of his hip pocket. He doesn't need an office so much as a living room, and at Global, that in effect is what he's got. He works best with a telephone or over lunch, and when he's hot − whether it's a matter of getting a story or lining up the backing for a new documentary series − he has a magic touch.

I once suggested to him that what he really needed to be a complete vice-president was a keeper, a high-powered executive and personal assistant, someone to follow him around with an appointment book, cigarettes, and a fistful of money. Cunningham endures that kind of comment stoically enough from me, but there are times, obviously, when it rankles.

"When I left the CBC," he told Barbara Byers of *Broadcaster* magazine, "I had the reputation of being a terrible administrator." But he pointed out that at Global in the previous two years he had cut half-hour unit costs by 34 per cent and had increased ratings by 70 per cent simultaneously. Hardly evidence of poor administration, he noted dryly.

Cunningham is the kind of man who can drive up to the main door of a downtown hotel, leave the keys in the ignition, stalk into the hotel without a backward glance, and never lose the thread of what he's trying to say. I've been with him in that scenario many times, and while Cunningham is talking, I'm in a panic about the car. I'm looking desperately over my shoulder for the doorman, and losing most of what Cunningham is saying.

He is prone to lard his conversation with expressions that appeal to him for a month or two. For a while, when he was getting the news service started and we were doing a great deal of talking about the future, it was what we would do "going down the road." For a time, "the bottom line" and "in a funny kind of way" got more than their share of the conversational work load. When he was trying to suggest a way of handling a story without actually dictating the content, it was "not those words, but that music." And any time we were cranking up the news service for a special effort, planning a high profile series of assignments that would give us an unwarranted bang for our bucks, it was the phrase, which gave me the title for this book, it was time for the "smoke and mirrors" again.

Cunningham has bursts of intense activity, followed by languid holding periods when one has difficulty getting his attention about anything more important than lunch. That's probably inevitable in someone who refuses to take a decent holiday. He has taken two that I know of since he began at Global. I remember a skiing holiday in Switzerland, which ended when a Global crew and I went to London and Belfast after the Provos gunned down eight people in County Armagh. Cunningham joined us in London, sans skis. He left us for what he thought was more holiday, a meeting in Germany with Albert Speer, Hitler's architect, industrial minister, and right-hand man, about the first film in our "Lives" series, "The Last Nazi." Cunningham has always found it difficult to distinguish between a holiday and an interesting bit of work, and most of the others are the same way.

But for all his flaws, all his peccadillos, he is very probably the best, most completely rounded news executive in the business. He is the only man for whom I have ever worked who not only knows exactly what I can do, but more important, exactly what I can't.

Don Cameron, the vice-president for News at CTV, is an old and valued friend of Cunningham's, with different strengths and different weaknesses. He maintains a boyish quality deep into middle age which charms most men and makes the opposite sex want to mother him. At the CBC, as a producer and an executive producer, Cameron was known as "Craze," and not always fondly. The label was due partly to a predilection for strong drink, since tamed, and partly because, when he was excited or angry about something, his normal conversation tone was halfway between a roar and a scream. He was and is one of the best producers of "crash" specials that this country has ever known. He got his early news training under Ab Gratton, at the Cornwall (Ont.) Standard-Freeholder in his home town. Gratton's list of graduates − among them Jim Purdie, Dick Brown, Burns Stewart − reads like a Who's Who of the media.

Cameron had a chequered career before he got to NBC News in New York. He had been a Navy flier, and I believe at one stage managed a supermarket or a grocery store. But television news entered his bloodstream at NBC and he never looked back. Like Cunningham, he knows the world better than most people know their own cities. He has a highly developed nose for news, and an ability to spot it when one of his own programs makes news. Cameron is one of the reasons that the Monday-morning papers often find themselves quoting "W-5" or "Question Period."

I first got to know Cameron in the early sixties, when he was a producer for CBC's "Newsmagazine," and I was the Washington correspondent for the *Montreal Star*. We had been working on the same story − the historic march on Washington which produced Dr. Martin Luther King's famous speech on the theme "I have a dream." When the march was over and we'd filed our stories, a group of us repaired to someone's hotel room for a drink.

Cameron was there, in full scream. He and his crew had just cut what they felt was a creditable "Newsmagazine." But a problem had developed in the live feed. It had gone straight to air in Canada from U.S. network facilities in Washington, and the American crew who handled the feed, clearly hadn't attached much importance to it.

Inadvertently, I had stumbled on what turned out to be a milestone dispute in the ten-year row between the director class and the journalists. While Knowlton Nash was talking about the peaceful restraint of the day's march, WTTG unbeknownst to David Marcus Roland, the director and the man in charge, was feeding its own pictures to the CBC. And what WTTG was carrying at that moment, was a historic documentary on previous Washington demonstrations, complete with "Wobblies," machine guns, pick-axe handles, and a lot of blood. In Toronto, it began to dawn on the great minds of the news service that there was some discrepancy between what Nash was saying and what the pictures were showing. The feed was going live to the CBC network, of course, and the fact that something was wrong was obvious much earlier to hundreds of thousands of puzzled viewers.

The foul-up came about as a direct result of the CBC division of authority between directors and journalists. Journalists like Cameron were not trusted enough to be their own producers. And so, when Cameron remonstrated with Roland about the need for a direct talk-line from the Washington control room to Toronto, Roland, in effect, told him to mind his own business. For someone like Cameron, who had learned TV news at NBC, it must have been doubly infuriating. At any rate, Roland had no talk-line, and when Toronto finally realized something was wrong, it took precious minutes, instead of seconds, to reach him and get WTTG to patch in the right pictures. Not for the first time, or the last time, Cameron offered to quit.

That night, as we partied on, Cameron suggested that I get him a job with the *Montreal Star*. Perhaps ten times in the course of the evening, Cameron offered his services to the newspaper as if it were a fresh, new thought, and I, apparently convinced it was a newly-minted idea, welcomed him aboard on behalf of my editors. Some of our colleagues were good enough to tell us about it the following day.

There was one senior CBC producer who used to dine out, quite literally, on his accounts of Cameron's exploits. It seemed hilarious at the time, but in retrospect the stories that enlivened the corporation's executive dinner tables probably finished Cameron as a serious contender at the CBC. The stories continued to dog him long after the fires had cooled and the exploits had ended.

In the early seventies, Cameron worked for me for a time as executive producer of CBC's Toronto Regional news, when I was the network news chief. Fortunately for the corporation, we had retired as hell-raisers by then, but we managed to do some pretty stupid things anyway.

Barbara Frum, who later proved with radio's "As It Happens" that she is one of the wittiest and most skilful interviewers in the business, was at that time the main public affairs component in the early evening news hour which Cameron re-named "Weekday." As usual, the public affairs and news elements in the show were engaged in open warfare and one of Cameron's first responsibilities, when he took the program over, was to arrange a cease-fire. To cut a long story short, he decided to do it by easing Frum into a more circumscribed role, and I, to my everlasting sorrow, let him do it. Barbara soon became disheartened and quit. That was our first accomplishment as a team and I wish I didn't have to share the credit for it.

A few months later, I quit myself as head of News and was attempting to freelance. Cunningham hired me back as a reporter and I found myself working for Cameron on "Weekday." But that relationship didn't last long, because Cameron had finally had it with the CBC, and he moved to CTV as the executive producer of their news service under his old friend Tom Gould.

Gould, then head of CBC News, had been the CBC's United Nations correspondent, when I first met him in New York. Like Cunningham and Cameron, he had had a stormy on-and-off-again relationship with the CBC. No one ever opposed CBC management for more of the right reasons. After he'd concluded an assignment to the Far East and the Vietnam war, he returned to

Canada and the CBC's Ottawa bureau, to continue the fight on home turf. He quit, finally, on a matter of principle. The annual Press Gallery dinner, as I've mentioned, is an off-the-record event. People drink too much, let their hair down, and say things they might later regret if revealed publicly. John Diefenbaker, who probably hadn't had anything to drink, but who understood that he was speaking in a private forum at the dinner that year, made some remark or other, I believe about his retirement. One of the CBC's spear carriers in the Gallery immediately phoned "The National," and the decision was made to carry the story, despite the traditional embargo. When Gould heard about this breach of ethics, he went berserk, and quit on the spot.

I didn't see much of Tom over the intervening years, but I had a nasty brush with him once on the telephone during the October Crisis in 1970. Tom carried, and I think continues to carry, a sizable chip on his shoulder about the CBC, and that was at the root of the trouble. I was pretty angry when I called him as the October Crisis was coming to an end. CBC cameras that afternoon were providing exclusive live coverage of that last ride of James Cross and his kidnappers into the arms of the authorities. Watchers in the CBC newsroom began yelling when suddenly the picture on the CTV monitor began to match ours. They were stealing our live transmission and broadcasting it with their own commentary.

But when I called Gould to remonstrate, I got a good deal worse than I gave. He denied nothing, but argued that we were a publicly supported institution and that we had no right to hog history-in-the-making. At that time, we were on different sides of the fence, and I had little sympathy for Gould's position.

Despite my differences with Gould, I have great respect for what he did at CTV. He fought for the right things, often against a board of directors who seemed to put their own interests and those of their stations ahead of those of the network. He tried desperately to get CTV News extended from its present sixteen minutes to something approaching twenty-five minutes, but he apparently couldn't get it past the CTV directors. On one occasion, CHAN-TV, the CTV station in Vancouver, refused to air a network special from Quebec on the grounds that Vancouver couldn't have cared less. Tom battled the directors on that one, but they rallied to their colleague at CHAN, and Tom lost. Shortly after that, discouraged and disillusioned, he quit as CTV's vice-president. He continued for a time with his "Backgrounder" to the news, but when his contract expired, CTV dropped that too.

What Gould managed to accomplish in his nine years as head of News and Current Affairs should not be forgotten. He started with practically nothing, and before he was finished he'd built up a reasonably respectable news service with some excellent correspondents; had nurtured "W-5's" big Sunday-night audience; had pioneered the early-morning show, "Canada AM;" launched "Maclear" – a success story on its own; had broken new ground with his own nightly comment, the first on a daily news program by a resident commentator; and had established, with Ken Lefoli and Jerry Lawton, the country's premiere documentary unit.

It is true that in the last months of his vice-presidency, he dropped the reins at least once, and then picked them up again, much to the consternation of Cameron, who was desperately trying to take up the slack without actually pushing Gould out of the driver's seat. Cameron is only now beginning to emerge from the wreckage of Gould's last months. The documentary unit has gone, to all intents and purposes, but "W-5" is on top again after the disastrous interlude with "CTV Reports," and I suspect that the 11:00 newscast will eventually do better than anyone expects with Nash as the face of the competition.

But Cameron marches to a different drummer than Gould. I don't think that he is the same kind of fighter that Gould used to be, or even that Cameron used to be.

I got a taste of the way the wind was blowing the day after I told him I was leaving "CTV Reports." Cameron took me and producer Andy Cochrane to lunch at La Scala, CTV's executive dining room, where, in a civilized fashion, they both tried to talk me out of leaving.

That was followed by a very different kind of session in Cameron's office, long after it had become apparent to him and everyone else that my mind was made up. We had been joined by Tim Kotcheff, newly appointed as Don's assistant, and Murray

Chercover, the CTV president. Kotcheff accused me of being a quitter, and Cameron, in a burst of unaccustomed nastiness, suggested I should get out of the business completely. The implication was that I didn't have what it took. I would have felt much better about the whole thing if I had been convinced that all this sudden passion and bluster was for my benefit. Clearly it was for Chercover's.

The incident revealed a Cameron so unlike the one I knew that I'm trying to forget it. I prefer to remember him in Vietnam, just before the fall of Saigon. As chief of CTV News, there was no real reason for Cameron to be there. But he had covered the Vietnam war so long, as a CBC producer, that he just couldn't stay away when it appeared that South Vietnam was about to go under.

Unlike Cunningham, Cameron has been able to get out of the office fairly frequently. He went to China in 1979, for example, to make arrangements for a new Peking bureau. And whenever there seems to be a lull in the unending night of the long knives at CTV, Cameron heads south, to the islands in the sun.

By all accounts, at least in terms of law and order, the best news chief that the CBC ever had was Denis Harvey, of *The Canadian* magazine, the *Montreal Gazette*, and now the *Toronto Star*, who succeeded Bill Cunningham the second time around. He was tough, knew his news, inspired respect and tightened discipline. But he was a print man, with no previous television experience, and I don't think he really understood what the Cunninghams were all about. Before he had a chance to understand, he was promoted.

Cliff Lonsdale, a recent head of News, or chief news editor as he is again known, was appointed to the executive ranks in 1976, and lasted until 1979. Lonsdale and I had worked briefly together as writers on the national desk, back in the late sixties. As I remember him he was a first-rate writer. He'd worked for various newspapers and news agencies in Zambia, Rhodesia, and the United Kingdom. And he'd worked in both radio and TV news, for both the CBC and the BBC. However, he seems to be no closer to solving a multitude of fifth-floor problems than the men who preceded him.

I hadn't had much to do with Lonsdale during my years at Global, but we had a brush with him on the federal election night, 1979, when I found myself in Tom Gould's old October Crisis position. We weren't doing full election-night coverage at Global. We had no budget for it. So we were contenting ourselves with short updates during the station breaks. As a result, we had no computer of our own, and were relying primarily on Canadian Press, which was slow, and the CBC, which was very quick.

Halfway through the evening, Cunningham got an angry phone call from Lonsdale, who had figured out what we were doing. He threatened to take action against us, unless we ceased and desisted. In my view he didn't have a leg to stand on, at least legally.

But to avoid giving Lonsdale heart failure, I suggested an alternative. On the questionable theory that if taking from one source could be called plagiarism then taking from two sources could be called research, I had the writers in the studio split the difference between the numbers the CBC computer was producing and numbers the CTV computer was turning out. From then on, right to the bitter end, Global's numbers were closer to the final result earlier than either the CBC's or CTV's.

In the light of my own reaction to Gould's theft of the Cross cavalcade pictures, I couldn't fault Lonsdale for his reaction to our larceny. But it seemed to me that he had a somewhat shrivelled sense of humour.

With or without a funny bone, Lonsdale was banished to London in December 1979, to do penance as the European supervisor of radio and television News and Current Affairs. He was replaced as chief news editor by Vince Carlin, age thirty-five, a native of Brooklyn, New York, and a graduate of Georgetown University and Time-Life Inc. Carlin was chief of *Time*'s Montreal bureau from 1970 to 1973, when he renounced Luce and joined the CBC.

When I was executive producer of "The National," Moses Znaimer was the boy wonder of Current Affairs. He interviewed me for a program he was doing on television news, and he asked me if I ever thought about the power I had as the straw boss of the country's leading newscast.

It was the kind of question that revealed as much about the interviewer as the interviewee. I don't remember how I answered him. Probably the same way I would now. You don't think about the power you have in a job like that, unless you're demented. You think about the responsibility. The more you think about the responsibility, the more you worry. And worry, constant worry, is the hallmark of a good newsroom.

We all do. Not just news executives, but the other inhabitants of the back room. Producers, deskmen, writers, field producers, cameramen, film editors, editorial assistants – everyone involved in a responsible editorial process. They are concerned less with power than with communication – with getting and telling a complex story accurately in its simplest terms.

There are signs that these communicators are the elite of the future, as the sociologists suggest. You see them, field producers and camera crews, thanks to their expense accounts, in the best hotels and restaurants all over the world. And they deserve it. They work incredible hours in difficult, often dangerous conditions. The best of them have very spotty family lives, for, like their bosses, the news must be everything. They used to be chosen people whose common denominators were hardship, stamina, skill, and bravery. In addition to that, now, they are just beginning to be an elite in terms of pay.

For every story you see on the evening news, there are at least a dozen people in back rooms, without whom the story could not have been aired. Global News is the tiniest network operation in the country (it may even be smaller than the newsrooms of some large stations) but we have about seventy people on the news staff in Toronto and Ottawa. And we draw on the services of many more from the production, technical, and managerial side of the Global operation.

As in most news services, there is one man under the chief news officer, the news director or executive producer, who manages the daily operation. He is responsible for implementing policy, for hiring and firing staff, for external relations (with the news services to which we subscribe, the clients who subscribe to our own service, and with the companies who control our means of transmission), and for internal relations, including staff scheduling.

Under him, there is a unit manager, budget chief, head accountant – call him what you will – who must keep track of how the money is being spent almost on a daily basis, and if necessary hit the warning buzzer, as it drifts inevitably into the red. There is never enough money, anywhere in this business, so the unit managers tend to be typecast as nay-sayers, or as President Johnson once described Republicans, "the wooden soldiers of the status quo."

The assignment editor, or assignment producer – the nomenclature varies – reports to the news director. His job is to juggle story ideas, reporters, camera crews, and to keep them all in the air, all day, until when the first newscast goes to air, they have dropped neatly into his hands and have lived up to everyone else's unreasonable expectations. It is, perhaps, the most thankless job in the business.

The assignment editor has got to be sure that the news service continues to break new ground, that we keep up to date on continuing stories, and that he maintains enough staff flexibility to cover the unexpected – a resignation, a shooting, a disaster, a domestic reaction to a startling piece of news from abroad. That means that he must keep track of all his people in the field, for every moment of every day, whether they're in Barrie, Ottawa, or Beirut, by radio, telephone, and, if necessary, cable. Most of the assignment editors I know seem to have a telephone growing out of their left ears, and a permanent line-up of people at their desks, who have got to get or deliver a vital piece of information immediately.

One of his major problems is that in television, he cannot risk drawing too many blanks on a given day. We must have pictures, and at Global, for each early newscast, we have at least eight of our own stories. We have an hour to fill with pictures, and we would not last long as a Canadian news service if the volume of U.S. network material became too heavy.

On a newspaper, a city editor or a news editor has a much larger available staff, and thus much greater freedom to make bad assignments. If the TV assignment editor guesses wrong, that is, if he has committed too many of the troops to the wrong stories, we wind up having to handle some important news stories as "on-camera" briefs. And in a television newscast, that tends to give them the wrong emphasis, too little emphasis. Because we are forced to put so many of our eggs in one basket, we find ourselves having to boil them whether or not they are broken. Stories that didn't work out, that have in the daily search and destroy process become non-stories, tend to make it to air anyway. Often we find we can't live without them.

It isn't enough that the assignment editor have good editorial sense, good story ideas to follow. He must be able to get what he asks for – or something better than that – from each reporter. He is, after all, in sole possession of the day's overview. And he must be firm about what he wants without being tyrannical about it. Reporters, even more than some of the other people in television news, tend to be creative and difficult, both sensitive and over-bearing stars-in-the-making. So if the reporters are going to handle stories in the way that the assignment editor in his wisdom wants them handled, he has to be prepared to brief each of them thoroughly, wheedle, and negotiate. And he has to live with the idea that stories do not always work out the way he wants them. The facts must be allowed to get in the way. The expression "wiped out," for me, describes the look on the average assignment editor's face at about 4:00 P.M. on the average day.

Adding to the assignment editor's woes is the fact that in most television operations, the line-up editor or producer, the man who structures the newscast for airing, is free to disagree with the assignment desk's judgement about the most important news of the day.

The fact that the assignment editor and the line-up editor are separate people has always seemed to me to be an unreasonable division of labour and responsibility. On a newspaper, for example, the city editor assigns stories, vets copy, and effectively places them in the paper. The TV line-up editor may find himself stuck with a reel-full of stories which do not reflect for him the most important news of the day.

Since he is responsible, ultimately, for giving the newscast its breadth, depth, and shape, this may present some difficulties. As air-time rushes inexorably closer, the pressure mounts. Throughout the day, he must stay on top of what is happening not simply in his own coverage area but around the world. He must know not just what his own reporters are covering, but what they are missing as well, for in the end, some items will have to be done as an anchorman voiceover with library film or as an ''on-camera'' brief. He must also know what visual items he can expect from the networks whose services his own organization subscribes to, and he must often base his judgements of those stories on two or three words in an advance line-up.

He must get his own tentative line-up – which lists the order of stories and briefs – out early, because that order will have a profound bearing on the way that reporters will handle their assignments, writers will introduce them, and the way that film and video tape editors will position them on the film reel or the news tape. Despite the tentative line-up, however, he must remain flexible.

Assigned stories will not always turn out to be as advertised on the daily outlook sheet. Some of them will not be available because the essential elements couldn't be filmed, or because the crew got caught in a traffic jam and film didn't make it to the lab in time for processing. The American news feeds, for some of the same reasons, do not always deliver as promised. And of course there is the ever-present factor that news will simply not stand still. Developing stories can be overtaken by events, and the big stories have an awkward habit of breaking ten minutes before air-time. The most careful line-up in the world can go into a last-minute tail spin.

Despite all of this certain uncertainty, he has to bring his sixteen-minute or twenty-five-minute or fifty-minute newscast out on time; precisely on time. He can live with being ten seconds light, perhaps, but if he is ten seconds heavy, and the announcer can't pick up the pace to bring him out on time, the line-up editor has to adjust on the fly. The need for precision means that changes have to be made constantly while the newscast is on the air. If a late feed is fifteen seconds longer than promised, fifteen seconds will have to come out of the newscast somewhere else. This causes inspired and not-so-inspired juggling with briefs, other short on-camera pieces and even visual items. If he's not deliberate and careful about this, he can make the anchorman's lot miserable.

Even in an organization where the anchorman does a lot of his own script, there is a need for news writers to help him put it together. One man could easily write a one-hour newscast if all the information were available even by mid-afternoon. But it never is. Stories are constantly changing, even while the newscast is on the air. If a newscast doesn't have the latest information, its content isn't news but current affairs.

Many of the briefs and introductions to film items (''intros,'' as they are known) are written early, in the hope that they will stand up until air-time. The world's time zones help, of course. If it's a European or Middle Eastern story that you're trying to intro for an early-evening newscast, chances are that it will be all wrapped up by 3:00 P.M. North American time. Newsmakers, like everyone else, need rest and sleep at the end of the day, and in Europe and the Middle East, which are from five to seven hours ahead, they are often in bed by air-time in Canada.

Despite the assist from the time zones, however, intros and briefs written too early may often have to be rewritten two or three times. Reporters routinely get back to the newsroom with just enough time to process the film, write and record a voice track, and edit the film. Often the reporter's script and suggested intro aren't available until an hour before air-time, say 5:00 P.M. Also at 5:00 P.M., at least in the Global newsroom, ABC begins its closed circuit news feed, on which we depend for most international items that will be run high in the newscast.

And so although one man, theoretically, could write the whole thing himself, in practice it simply isn't possible. Too much information, visual and otherwise, comes flooding into the newsroom during the same brief period. At Global, we routinely go to air with several blank pages in the script, representing briefs and intros yet to be written.

Often, because the ABC news service reserves the best of the day's visual items for its evening newscast, and that isn't available until 6:00 P.M., at the same time we are on the air, we have to do what we call a fast turnaround. We record the ABC item on our VTR machines, put electronic cues on its top and tail, and run it back into our own newscast perhaps two minutes later. In that short period, one of the writers will have to write or at least rework an intro that will set the item up properly, and be sure that everyone who needs copies gets them – the anchorman, the line-up editor, the director, the script assistant, the man in the sound booth, and last but not least, the person who is running the electronic idiot card, the auto cue, the machine that allows the anchorman to maintain eye contact with the viewer as he reads, and give the impression that he's memorized what he's saying. There's no smoke from the auto cue. It's all done with two-way mirrors, literally.

Now and then we do what is known as a hot switch. We ascertain in advance, as closely as possible, exactly where ABC plans to use a given item in its newscast. If ABC's time estimate is out, the anchorman will have to be prepared to chop off his intro early, or spin it out a little longer, until the ABC item is available. The intro must make sense, shortened or lengthened, because the item must be taken live and clean, without clipping the top of the item and without having the unexplained face of the U.S. anchorman, who is at that moment reading his intro, pop briefly into the Global newscast. Or at least that's the theory. It's at times like that that an anchorman reflects how good it would be to work for an organization with money. If you work for CBS, you don't have to suffer the indignity of that kind of Russian roulette.

Getting good writers, who can operate under that kind of pressure, is not easy, and keeping them is even tougher. Night after night of grinding out snippets, without ever really getting your teeth into anything or writing script which the anchorman may decide arbitrarily he can't read, is not what most of us went into news for in the first place. In the event that some miniature masterpiece is dropped, it is useless to point out to the anchorman that he himself wrote and read something in a similar vein the night before. If the anchorman isn't comfortable with it, at that moment, it has to go, at least at Global.

It can be a rewarding job, but only if the writer realizes how difficult it really is to do it well. Writers are most often recruited from the newspapers and wire services, and this is one of the best ways of breaking into television news. The new writer soon finds that the most effective weapon in the armoury is the simple, declarative sentence. Television writers have to avoid the choppy adjectival pile-up that is the hallmark of newspaperese. They have to write sentences that read smoothly, have a nice balance, and finish strongly. A spoken sentence cannot simply trail off into space. Good television news writing is a mixture of dramatic monologue and blank verse.

A good intro must put the film or tape story which follows it into context and at the same time tease it, that is, stimulate the viewers' interest in what's next. It must provide a news peg, a reason for the upcoming story, and it must give the viewer no alternative but to watch and listen. It is these nuances which make the difference between a merely acceptable writer and a good one.

George Wolff, at Global, is consistently the best news writer I have ever encountered. He writes simply and cleanly. He is not above a play on words, but he doesn't debase the currency by indulging himself too frequently. He doesn't reach. He understands that in television the right word in the right place can and often must do the work of a whole sentence. He does not underestimate the difficulty of what he's trying to do. Show me someone who thinks that writing an intro is easy, and I'll show you someone who turns out pedestrian work.

George made it the hard way. When I first went to the CBC, George was a copy clerk. He bought a simple camera with his own money and began shooting news film on spec in his spare time. He got little encouragement from mother corporation. While I was still in a position of some authority, a job opened up for an assistant cameraman, a trainee, in some other alley of the CBC labyrinth. I wrote a letter to the supervisor concerned, suggesting that he give George a hearing. George told me later that the man was cavalier about his application. He giggled at George throughout the interview.

When I left the CBC, George was still a copy clerk, but by this time, because of his obvious ability, he was on almost permanent "temporary upgrades." In the summer holiday period, he was writing for the CBC's national newscasts, and now and then he was actually acting as a line-up editor. When Global got under way, Cunningham quickly offered George a job. George has developed into one of the most valuable people in the Global operation. He can do just about any job in the newsroom. He can produce, line-up, write, and report. The problem is that like most of us, he prefers reporting.

In the end, a newscast is only as good as its back-up staff. Editorial assistants, or copy clerks, tear off and distribute the copy from the wire machines, haul gallons of coffee, run off and distribute line-ups, look after supers (names, dates, and additional information which is superimposed on the TV picture), run errands, "split" scripts (that is, separate and distribute the six-page carbon copy books on which most scripts are written), run the auto cue, and otherwise ground themselves for a career in news. Too often, their jobs are a dead end, and most of them know it.

Theoretically, the line-up editor, or producer, is in charge of the newscast until he hands the completed script to the director, the man who actually calls the shots for getting the newscast on the air in its prescribed form. From that moment on, in most TV news operations, there is a division of authority. The producer continues to dictate what he wants, but the director makes the technical decisions which will determine whether he gets it.

Good news directors are rare. They are now the chief technical practitioners of live television. Almost every other kind of programming these days, except news specials and sports, is on film or tape. Newscasts have always been live, and will continue to be, except for film and tape inserts, for obvious reasons. If you taped a newscast, by the time you had aired it it would no longer be news, but history.

Being a good news director requires an ability to think on your feet, to keep your head while all about you are losing theirs, and to be ready, instantly, for anything. For most newscasts, there is little or no rehearsal. There isn't time for that. And in addition, there is a widespread conviction that news should be pure and somewhat breathless, that rehearsing it makes it show business, somewhat fraudulent, and a little demeaning.

The director must be ready for film breaks, for example. If that happens, he has three choices. He can instruct the anchorman to read "on-camera" copy. He can, at least on the commercial networks, tell the anchorman to "throw" to commercial. Or he can call for the intro to the next tape item on his line-up. He cannot, under any circumstances, call for the next film item, because the break means that the film reel, on which film items are spliced together in order of appearance, is now in two pieces. And whatever he does, he must do it in a way that doesn't compound the sloppiness which has already been displayed to the viewer.

Once a film breaks, or a tape machine fails to "lock up," and the director is arbitrarily forced to change the line-up, the possibility of trouble, fresh trouble, is tripled. If disaster is to be averted, the director must be a good communicator. He has to make sure that everyone involved in the airing of the newscast − the script assistant, the switcher, the sound man, the film chain operator, the VTR operator, the studio director, the studio cameraman, the auto cue operator, the anchorman − knows that the line-up has been changed and how it has been changed. If one team member gets confused, more disaster is imminent. On a live newscast, trouble is like a snowball rolling downhill.

The director's right arm is the script assistant, sometimes called a production assistant. He or she (usually she) must have a clock for a brain. It's little use knowing how much time has elapsed in a newscast. What she must be aware of constantly is how much time is left. What this means is that she must constantly "backtime," like a computer, so that she can tell the director at any point in the newscast whether he is running twenty seconds light (in which case he will run out of newscast ten seconds too soon) or whether he is a minute and thirty seconds heavy (which means that the anchorman is likely to be overtaken by a station break before he's finished). A script assistant can make all the difference between a clean, easy newscast, or a choppy, difficult one that makes the viewers as nervous as the participants. That is why a good one is treasured, and credited at the end of a newscast, not because, as Dennis Braithwaite once suggested, she might be interesting in bed.

A newscast needs a good technical producer – the man who knows how to call up back-up systems or suggest jury rigs in the event of trouble – a good soundman, who must open the right pot, that is, turn up the correct volume control for all his separate sources of sound: film, tape, remote, or studio. It also needs a good switcher.

As the man in the sound booth is responsible for selecting the right sounds on the director's cue, the switcher must select the right pictures. He sits in the control room beside the director. In front of him is an array of monitors and a complex switching panel with a number of "busses," which allow him to cut from camera one (the anchorman's main camera) to VTR picture, for example, or dissolve from film, at the end of a moving item, to the anchorman reacting in the studio. He is responsible for "keying," that is, putting two pictures together electronically. The little graphics you see beside an anchorman's head are not really where they appear to be. They are often on camera cards, being shot in another studio. The anchorman sits in front of a background of a distinctive hue called "chromokey" blue. The switcher can make anything that is that precise colour of blue disappear, thus the anchorman who appears with graphics can be chromokeyed over the graphic card in another room. The switcher's job is complicated, and has to be performed with blinding speed and precision. Sometimes, in planning his next step, his flickering fingers stray, and at times like that, an anchorman can pop up inexplicably in the middle of a film item.

The studio cameramen have to be able to move quickly too. Most newscasts are a three-camera operation. There is one camera for the graphics stand, another that does triple duty on graphics, newsroom signature shots, and performers, and a third that does double duty, as the main anchor camera and for other performers, like the sports editor, who sit in. The cameras are heavy brutes and sometimes there are only a few seconds in which to move them, refocus them, and reframe the shot. Although being a studio cameraman on a news show is not likely to satisfy a serious cameraman for very long it requires dedication, attention, and a cool head.

The key man in the studio, perhaps, is the floor director. Although the anchorman usually has a telex link with the control room (the tiny earpiece you sometimes glimpse in his ear), his main link is through the floor director, who tells him what to do, with a series of hand signals, when an audio instruction through his telex, barked while he is taking a breath, might throw him off his script. The floor director is responsible for keeping the performer informed about the amount of time remaining before the newscast goes to air, for cueing him to start speaking when it does go on the air, for directing him to the live camera when more than one is in operation, for turning him from one camera to another if the format demands it, to count him down to films and tapes, to speed him up or slow him down, and to get him off the air with little or no egg on his face.

It is a job in which personality is vital. A cheerful and relaxed but efficient floor director contributes visibly to a good newscast. One who is sour, tense, unorganized, abrasive, and prone to sudden, panicky hand signals, can turn a good newscast into ruins.

But all of this, the combined efforts of the vice-presidents, the executive producer, the assignment and line-up editors, the writers, the editorial assistants, the people in the control room and on the studio floor, go for naught unless the reporters, the cameramen, and sometimes the field producers have delivered the stories.

CHAPTER SEVEN

The Television News Story

The viewer might well suppose that the last place he'd hear an inconclusive debate about what news is and what it isn't is in a television newsroom. But nowhere that I know of does the argument rage more fiercely.

News is a spectator sport for most people. They are not participants, and although they often have their own strenuous opinion about the way a newspaper or a newscast has handled a story, their relationship to the news of the day is essentially reactive, if not almost passive. Getting new people in the business to trade in their bystanding instincts for an active news gathering outlook is one of the most difficult tasks we face.

In my own early days as a reporter for the *Ottawa Journal*, I learned that lesson, or rather began to learn it, the hard way. My father was then the head of The National Film Board, which at the time was just beginning to do things for television.

My father authorized the purchase of perhaps a dozen television sets for his key production people, so that they could keep an eye on NFB programming at home. However, the Treasury Board got wind of it, and ordered that the sets be removed to the appropriate offices and kept there. The Board did not object to the idea that senior people should be able to watch their own programming. But it was somehow sinful of them to want to do it at home.

I mentioned this over a drink in the Ottawa Press Club one day, in the midst of a conversation about the wilful unreasonableness of the Treasury Board. I was horrified to read about it the next day on the front page of the opposition newspaper, the *Ottawa Citizen*.

Like most neophytes, I had been too close to the story to see it. I couldn't have pursued the story myself for the *Journal*, because it would have betrayed a domestic confidence and caused problems for my father. But if I had recognized it as news in the first place, I wouldn't have babbled about it in the Press Club in front of an opposition reporter who felt no such constraints.

That is one reason why a newsman can never simply work an eight-hour shift. To become part of the news process, he has to accept the fact that news occurs constantly throughout the twenty-four hours of a day, sometimes under his nose, sometimes oceans away. News doesn't happen in the newsroom, but outside it, and for its inhabitants, that is sometimes surprisingly easy to forget. The average human runs into an impressive quantity of interesting and unpublished material that qualifies as news in the course of a lifetime. Some of it is simply in the realm of "human interest." Sometimes it's much harder than that, leaked inadvertently by someone like me, who was too close to the forest to see the trees. Newsmen have to work consciously at seeing the trees. Some of them are better at it than others. Personally, I am still trying to rise above an inauspicious beginning.

The shorter Oxford describes news as "tidings; new information of recent events; new occurrences as a subject of report or talk." I think that's accurate as far as it goes, but it fails to take into account the fact that since the beginning of time, most of the "tidings" have been bad.

Barbara Tuchman, in the foreword to her enthralling work on the fourteenth century, *A Distant Mirror,* cites some of the problems faced by the social historian. One problem, of course, is that after several decades or several centuries, there are great gaps in the surviving information.

"A greater hazard," she writes, "built into the very nature of recorded history, is overload of the negative: the disproportionate survival of the bad side − of evil, misery, contention, and harm. In history, this is exactly the same as in the daily newspapers. The normal does not make news. History is made by the documents that survive, and these lean heavily on crisis and calamity, crime and misbehaviour, because such things are the subject matter of the documentary process – of lawsuits, treaties, moralists' denunciations, literary satire, papal Bulls. No Pope ever issued a Bull to approve of something. . . ''

I am overly fond of that passage perhaps because it puts the blame at least for unpleasant history squarely on the shoulders of those who deserve it – the shoulders of lawyers, politicians, preachers, do-gooders, essayists, and Popes. But newsmen do not get off scot free. Ms. Tuchman properly shoots us down for failing to put the bad news in context:

''Disaster is rarely as pervasive as it seems from the recorded accounts. The fact of being on the record makes it appear continuous and ubiquitous whereas it is more likely to have been sporadic in time and place. Besides, persistence of the normal is usually greater than the effect of disturbance, as we know from our own times. After absorbing the news of today, one expects to see a world consisting entirely of strikes, crimes, power failures, broken water mains, stalled trains, school shutdowns, muggers, drug addicts, neo-Nazis and rapists. The fact is that one can come home in the evening – on a lucky day – without having encountered more than one or two of these phenomena.''

Unfortunately, the general public seems to forget that the human race has always taken the good news for granted while it was faithfully recording calamity. The man on the street also tends to confuse the messenger with the message. A stranger recognized me not so long ago in some public place and after confirming my identity, suggested sternly that I had better mend my ways because the viewers had had just about all the bad news they were going to stand for.

A fourteen-year-old viewer sent me the perfect answer to that testy stranger, but like most good answers, it arrived too late. The answer, ascribed to one John C. Keenan, had been copied out of an old *Reader's Digest*.

''It is pointless to complain that crime and sin receive more publicity than exemplary behaviour,'' Keenan wrote. ''It is, on the contrary, a matter of some satisfaction that sin is still regarded as news. It will be a sad day if integrity and goodness become so rare as to be featured in the newspapers.''

The truth is that most people enjoy bad news, as long as the bad news is about someone else, in which case one is prompted to count his blessings. And if the bad news affects everyone, it promotes a sense of fellowship in distress. Then too, bad is how you see it. It used to be a standing joke in the Global newsroom that when Ken Mallett, then the executive producer, was smiling, it was a safe bet that someone, somewhere in the world, was in serious trouble, and that we were going to have film or tape of that trouble by 6:00 P.M.

Good news is not all that easy to come by. And we have to face the fact that news is the aberration, not the norm. People just aren't interested in the fact that 42,000 cars made it across a level railway crossing without incident; that 900 airplanes landed safely at their destination; that a politician declared himself in favour of mother-hood; that two countries have no intention whatever of going to war; or that 600 famous and well-loved octogenarians made it through one more day without heart failure.

I think that part of the reason for the current outcry against bad news is what Harry Boyle has identified as the public's new perception of its rights, inspired by television. After the advent of the daily newspaper, the English-speaking world, at least, came to believe that it had a right to information. Television has prompted people to believe that they have a new right, which overshadows the old one: the right to entertainment.

I think that is one reason that the newspapers, magazines, and newscasts are being taken to task for the bad news they purvey. But the truth of the matter is that we're not printing or broadcasting enough bad news. We have begun to react to those who want stories with happy endings, who want the bad news to be in manageable proportions, or, who, if the bad news is larger in scope, want it in small doses so that the whole distressing picture is not readily apparent.

They do not want to hear the whole truth about the state of the nation or the western world, and when they are forced to listen too often, they lash out, not at the politicians or themselves, but at the messengers. By and large, if they don't want to hear it, they won't listen and if they have to listen they do not have to believe it. The

American refusal to accept the reality of the energy crisis in the first half of 1979 is a case in point.

The exercise of news judgement may well be the least empirical process since Orville Wright learned to fly after he was in the air. Although no two newsmen anywhere agree completely on what is news, hence the unending arguments in the newsroom, they would probably agree that in developing news judgement, there is no substitute for experience.

There is danger, however, in the fact that we learn from trial and error. Error, in the exercise of news judgement, can be said to be missing a story that one of your competitors didn't. What this tends to mean is that you rely on the judgement of your peers as to whether or not you made a mistake. In a television operation, the herd instinct promotes undue reliance on the Canadian Press and the local dailies for determining what news should be covered on that day.

It is much more responsible to bring your own mind to bear on the events of the day and to conclude in the end that news is what you say it is. News can only be what interests newsmen. News is events that excite their imaginations.

I once suggested to a group of academics that news is what I can hardly wait to tell my wife when I get home at night. One of them astutely pointed out that I might also have been describing gossip. I could only defend myself by saying that Global News is not the sort of organization that accepts unchecked rumours of a personal nature as news, although I would not be prepared to swear in a court of law that we have never done so. And, in any event, there is an overlap between news and gossip that cannot be denied.

Global, like most other Canadian news organizations, reported in some detail the sordid pronouncements of that former flower child, Margaret Trudeau. In so doing, most newsmen took refuge in the assertion that politicians were public figures and that their private lives were not their own; or that since the aggrieved spouse in this instance was the Prime Minister of Canada, his wife's behaviour might be expected to have some damaging impact on the affairs of state.

127

I reject those notions. In the first place, I am convinced that politicians and other figures do have a right to privacy. Since when does mere visibility put one in the debt of the beholder? In the second place, I cannot for a moment imagine that if Margaret's conduct distressed the Prime Minister, and affected his public performance, that the salacious reporting of every mindless episode in any way contributed to his stability in office. As a matter of fact, it was recognized by Trudeau's associates that the public humiliation of the ''Margaret business'' so preoccupied the Prime Minister that there were periods when the country was without effective leadership.

We reported the Margaret stories at Global, not because we felt it was necessarily the only responsible thing to do. As a matter of fact, some of us came to wonder if it hadn't been irresponsible. Finally, we reported them simply because they were irresistible pieces of human drama, the stuff of which history is made. The plot and the characters were worthy of Shakespeare. Prince Hamlet, slowly going mad, wandering the ramparts of Elsinore. A maid, the fair Ophelia, cooing high-pitched non-sequiturs and dabbling her white hand in the babbling brook. The tragedy of a middle-aged man in a demanding job marrying someone almost half his age. No story teller – and that's what we are, the linear descendants of wandering minstrels and town-criers – could possibly have left it alone.

There is no magic formula for determining when gossip becomes news. No yardstick by which you can measure taste. I felt it was necessary to report, with as straight a face as possible, that President Nixon had once referred to Prime Minister Trudeau as ''an asshole.'' And I don't think we could or should have covered the Vietnam war protests in the United States without using the chant which summed up the whole movement, unbleeped and unexpurgated: ''One, two, three, four, we don't want your fucking war.''

But language is only a minor facet of taste, and taste is only a footnote in the ethics of journalism. Do you broadcast film of a correspondent being shot to death in cold blood by a Nicaraguan national guardsman? If so, why? Do you interview the bereaved parents of schoolboys who have drowned on a canoeing expedition? And if so, at what point does the public's right to know become an invasion of the individual's right to privacy? In my view, these questions and most of the others that arise on a daily basis in most newsrooms, have to be dealt with separately, on their merits.

For example, you publish pictures of ABC's Bill Stewart being gunned down in Nicaragua because it demonstrates in an unforgettable way the realities of a totalitarian regime. Events don't take place in a vacuum. The Somoza-controlled Nicaraguan press had for months been publishing stories which painted all the foreign critics, particularly the correspondents, as the tools of communism. To a young Nicaraguan national guardsman, frightened for his life, Bill Stewart was an acknowledged enemy. From his viewpoint, it wasn't so much a murder as a state execution. So we broadcast those heart-rending pictures of Stewart's death because it represented the truth, and because Bill Stewart would have died in vain if the networks had catered to people's sensibilities. To some extent, Bill Stewart's death is the reason that Somoza is gone.

You interview the parents and classmates of schoolboys who have drowned on a canoe trip because you can't simply tell people about agony and expect them to feel it. You have to show them what it is, and hope that this school and other schools and all the people who from time to time have our children in their keeping are moved to tighten up their systems so that this kind of thing can't happen again.

In reviewing a career, which has been studded with mistakes, I find that I regret the stories I didn't air or publish more than some of the ones I did. Insofar as the laws of libel and fair play allow, I think we serve the public best by delivering as many of the facts as possible and not standing between the viewers and the events we're covering as self-appointed censors. We are much more likely to find ourselves playing God in an act of suppression.

As Cunningham puts it, it is often necessary in the news business to "paint with broad strokes." Simplify it, but make it part of the larger landscape. Without a sense of the drama of news, it can't be done. A reporter who never feels the hair rise on the back of his neck when he is covering a big story would be better off as a bank clerk. But even while covering smaller stories, he has got to see how they fit into the scheme of things, why it matters in the context of our changing times, what it means to ordinary people. He has got to have historical perspective, or it ends up as another of those unconnected ''bitsy, piecey'' items that Harry Boyle so deplores.

To me, the most challenging jobs in the business are those of the television reporter and, because he is an integral part of the process, the news cameraman. The finished product is the work of a lot of people, but it begins with those two. If they, and in some instances the soundman and the field producer, don't come up with the facts and the pictures, it's all over before it begins.

A first-rate television reporter or correspondent is a very rare individual. First of all, of course, he has to be a good reporter. He has to have a nose for a story, insatiable curiosity and the stamina to feed it. He has to be fast and accurate about the stories he uncovers. He has to love the language and be able to use it. He has to know something about film directing and editing, and through it all, he must have the lofty eye of a producer. He must be a performer. All the other skills are wasted if he cannot lift a good line off the paper and deliver it into a microphone. He must be something of a ham, comfortable in front of a camera, because if he is nervous, it is quickly transmitted to the viewer.

To do an intelligent story in a minute and thirty seconds, an average length for a TV news item, the television reporter should know a good deal more about the story than his newspaper counterpart. If he doesn't, the story is likely to be as shallow as its length would appear to dictate. The television reporter, unlike his colleague on a newspaper, has only one chance to be right. If a newspaperman fails to isolate the most important elements in the story and get them into his lead paragraphs, he has a chance to recover. His emphasis may be wrong, but he will probably have included the important features whose significance he failed to realize while he was writing the story somewhere in the body of the piece. An alert deskman can still save his bacon, by spotting the real news, and moving it up to the top of the story.

The television reporter, on the other hand, is dead if he misses the salient features not just before he has written his script but while he is still on location. In newspaper terms, he really only has the headline and the equivalent of the first few paragraphs to tell the story. If he fails to isolate the guts of it on the spot, chances are he won't get covering film. And the deskman cannot save him, beyond using the information he missed in the intro, and making the reporter and his report look somewhat off-target, somewhat also-ran. A television story, because it is a complex mixture of picture and sound, on which it relies the way a newspaper relies on type, cannot be restructured easily.

If he is certain about his facts, certain that he has located the nub of the story, he can begin to make the film, the sound, and his own performance speak volumes. It is uncertainty and unorganized thought that puts viewers to sleep.

The much abused interview "clip" provides a case in point. A clip, in news terms, is a short section of speech or interview which should be used more than anything else to convey the flavour of the speaker, or his key thought, or because it is colourful, to punch up the story where it needs it. If an interview clip is used because the reporter isn't clear about the facts or the points that the interviewee is trying to make, it may be safe but it's also likely to be boring. And if the reporter, who was able to listen to the interview several times, isn't clear about the point that's being made, what hope is there for the viewer, who gets only one chance, while his or her faculties are at a low ebb after a hard day's work and he or she is easing the pain in a comfortable chair in the living room?

If a picture can in fact be worth a thousand words, the reporter must choose the right picture to depict the thousand words that he's trying to convey. If it's the wrong picture, or if the words he is trying to say over it in his script are in conflict with it, the message is going to be lost. It is an established fact of script writing that when the words and the pictures do not complement each other, the pictures usually win.

A good example of television's most common failing is the so-called "economic story." Too often, reporters try to illustrate such stories with pictures that are only vaguely appropriate, known in the business as "wallpaper." The reporter "cross scripts" such footage, that is, he talks about an impending auto strike over stock film of an automobile production line, so that the words really run across the visual thrust of the pictures. Unsupported by graphics or superimposed statistics which make the pictures secondary, that sort of item often falls apart. In the case of the strike story, the viewer tends to lose the thread of the report completely, and tries to figure out the make and year of the cars on the assembly line.

If you can't remember a story like that one, try the stories about the consumer price index, wheat sales, or pulp and paper production. Most viewers don't really hear why the consumer price index is up, how many bushels of grain we've sold to the Soviet Union, or what's happening to the pulp and paper industry. He gets instead a soporific impression of supermarket aisles and price tags, waving fields of wheat, or trees crashing to the ground, with the annoying buzz of a reporter off camera delivering dry facts in an unenlightening way. Most of us, at home and in the studio, can hardly wait until these stories are over. The difference is that in the studio we can't very well head for the refrigerator.

Thus, one of the cardinal rules: the script must fit the pictures, precisely. In a sense, a script should be written like a good newspaper cutline, the lines of explanation that appear under a still picture. A cutline which shows Joe Clark kissing a baby in an election campaign, should not relate what is obvious in the photo. It should take it a stage further, perhaps by saying when and where the picture was taken, and what Clark said to the baby's mother before he put his lips to the offending creature.

In television terms, it would be pointless to say over the film equivalent of that picture that Clark was kissing a baby; and it would be lost completely if you said that a short time earlier Clark had proposed tax cuts which could be expected to stimulate the Gross National Product by 5 per cent. You might conceivably get away with it, if you tied that information to the picture; if you said that while Clark was wooing babies he had not forgotten the rest of us, that he had offered tax cuts to stimulate the country's economic growth.

If he is skilful, a reporter's power to communicate is enormous, almost dangerously so. A pregnant pause can speak volumes. What he doesn't say can become significant if he leads the viewer right up to a conclusion and abandons him at the front gate. The right word, in the right place, can be made to provide a whole paragraph of explanation. The urgency of his voice, a facial expression, a gesture, the way he's standing, can colour a whole story.

But the reporter can do none of those things without the news cameraman, whose skills, in the right combination, are as rare as those of a good correspondent. It goes without saying that he must be a superb technician. Focus, exposure, use of the zoom, lighting, sound levels, must be second nature, so that he can think through the viewfinder. He must have lightning reflexes, because news only happens once. He must have iron nerves, because he must keep on rolling film despite the fist being waved in front of his lens, or the train that seems to be running into his left shoulder. He must trust his correspondent or his field producer, because while he's shooting he loses peripheral vision, and is completely blind to what is under his feet and behind him. He must trust one of them to keep him from tripping over a log or stepping backwards off the roof of a building. And he's got to be subtle. There are times when he must keep rolling unobtrusively, not to deceive newsmakers, but to avoid distracting them, to preserve the reality of the moment.

He must be able to edit in his head. He must know instinctively when to stop tracking a tank, for example, and let it roll out of frame. If the pan is too long, or the zoom isn't fast enough and smooth enough, his film may wind up on the cutting-room floor. He must be sure to shoot "cutaways," shots that allow the film editor to make smooth transitions. He's got to know the story as well as the correspondent does and be alert for symbolism. A shot of a crying child in the middle of a rocket bombardment can tell the whole story.

It is a wise correspondent or field producer who keeps the cameraman informed of his every thought as the story develops. You can't separate the editorial thrust of a story and its pictures. The reporter and field producer must be careful not to

133

develop the story too far independently, otherwise they may get back to the studio with a story for which they have no film, or film for which there is no story.

The most seasoned teams can make mistakes. I remember once at the CBC sending a crew to cover the aftermath of a plane crash. Department of Transport investigators were looking for the so-called black box, the flight recorder, hoping it would give them some sort of clue as to what had happened. They finally found the box, but the crew didn't. They came back to the newsroom with excellent film of the site – twisted wreckage, probing investigators, the pathos of strewn luggage. But they didn't have a single frame of the focal point of the story, the flight recorder. The story could not be used.

Some of the more affluent TV news operations use soundmen in their film operations. With the sound taken care of, the cameraman can concentrate fully on picture, without wondering whether his sound recording level is riding dangerously high, or if he turned the pot down so low when the artillery was firing that he isn't getting any sound at all as the gun crew stacks spent casings. But at Global, and many other smaller operations in North America, we use the CP 16 film camera, whose recording gear is built compactly into the camera. The sound is recorded directly on the film, which has a magnetic stripe, like a tiny audio tape, running along the unperforated edge. The microphone is placed on a quick-draw mount on top of the camera, aimed in the same direction as the lens. It can be whipped off quickly and hand-held if the reporter needs to do an interview.

There are other advantages to shooting sound-on-film. The most significant is that because the sound is being recorded frame by frame with the picture, there is no need to synchronize picture and sound, by using a light-buzzer combination, or a clapper board, before shooting, as there is with so-called double-system film. That can be a terrible nuisance on a fast-breaking story, although if you haven't got time to sync the shot at the top, you can also do it at the tail.

Most television news operations also use a field producer, to work with the reporter and camera crew at every stage of the story. There are advantages to this system, of course, if you are dealing with inexperienced reporters, or people like anchormen, whose skills in the field may have atrophied, or which may never have been fully developed in the first place.

One of the most important things Bill Cunningham has done at Global is to initiate the use of field producers and staff camera crews to get solid, local reporting out of southern Ontario's small towns and rural communities. Like most good ideas, this one seemed simple. But the concept was little short of brilliant.

The normal Canadian procedure for covering stories outside the big production centres is to staff them with a reporter and a crew from the central newsroom. The practice can lead to distortion and inaccuracy because it is essentially a hit-and-run operation. The reporter is handed a story idea – perhaps in the form of a clipping from the local newspaper, a piece of wire copy, or even a briefing from the assignment editor, who may have had a tip from someone on the spot. He augments that information as best he can, from his own files, by talking to a colleague who has had some experience in the area, or from the newsroom's own morgue or clipping library. Then he gets into the cameraman's car and he goes.

If he's smart, when he finally arrives at the scene of the story, he will talk not only to the principals, but if he has time, will also drop into the local newspaper or radio station, to pick up local colour and context.

But unless he's dedicated and lucky, or it's a simple, straightforward story, he's likely to make mistakes in fact and emphasis that will either amuse or annoy the people who are actually living with the story.

To avoid this traditional pitfall, Cunningham initiated the idea of "regional correspondents," a television adaptation of the newspaper "stringer" system. Like stringers, the regional correspondents are paid by the item. They keep watch for us on the local news scene, alerting us every time they think there is a local story brewing which has something more than local interest. If the regional field producer, who tries to keep his own tabs on the outlying areas by reading a stack of local dailies and weeklies, agrees that there is a story in the regional correspondent's suggestion, he meets him on the spot with a crew.

Thus, the editorial thrust of our regional stories is purely local. The regional correspondent, who usually works for a local newspaper or radio station, is not parachuted into the story. He lives and works in the region where he is exercising his journalistic curiosity. What he is missing, of course, is television expertise, or at least the ability to do the story cleanly and professionally for network viewing. The field producer and the Global crew provide the expertise, at one swoop, ensuring the editorial integrity of the piece, and network acceptability. This is the main reason that much of Global's ex-urban coverage has been so effective.

But there are other times, in my view, when the field producer tends to muddy the waters. Great journalism has rarely if ever been produced by committees. "Producerism" is what American correspondents began to call it in the 1960s. To them, it represented a reversal of the time-honoured journalistic roles, in which the reporter was the man who sniffed out the skeletal outline of a story, put flesh on it with hard work, and then delivered it in his own way to his home newsroom and ultimately to the audience. As television newscasts began to grow in length and importance, and reaching audiences became paramount, there was a shift in emphasis. Production values began to outweigh editorial values. Producers began to play a larger and larger role in exploiting the drama in news film.

It was a change in emphasis that was detected very early by the people seeking publicity. The public relations men in government began to call the producers first, not the reporters, and outline story ideas to them. Story ideas began to appear on assignment sheets with the notation, "talent to be assigned," an indication that the reporter was viewed more and more as a performer, and less and less as a working journalist. It was a development, which, while it lasted, interfered seriously with the reporting process and American standards. "Producerism," or "field-producerism," has never been as deeply entrenched in Canada, and for that we can be thankful, although Bill Cunningham might not agree.

I have worked with field producers a number of times, and about all that can be said for that arrangement from my point of view is that they're invariably good company and their presence makes the job easier and safer. It is easier because the correspondent has to worry about fewer details. He can forget about drivers, cars, passes, visas, airline schedules, film shipments, editing, satellite feeds, and the other nuts and bolts. If he's not careful, though, he can also find himself forgetting about the story. It's safer having a field producer, because two sets of news ganglia are always better than one. With a field producer, you are less likely to miss something. And, if you are rusty or inexperienced, or both, having a field producer holding your hand will at least ensure that the story you finally file will meet acceptable minimums.

But it may also ensure that the story is not really your own. It is the field producer, who, by directing the shooting and cutting of film, determines the story line, who echoes Cunningham, in effect, by saying "not those words, but that music." The reporter, of course, remains responsible for the facts and the script, but since, in a good television news story, picture and script are indivisible, he no longer has complete control over what he is saying. The problem is that in an industry where costs are so high, a guaranteed minimum often seems preferable to editorial purity.

No figures are available, but I would guess that CBC television news spends something like $50 million per year on its news operation. CTV News, I would estimate, spends somewhere between a fifth and a quarter of that amount. Global News, despite the fact that no other Canadian broadcaster commits as high a percentage of its total operating budget to news, has less than a tenth of the CBC's money.

With care, we can shoot the average news story on a 400-foot roll of film, but the last time I checked, raw filmstock was worth $50 per roll and rising. Processing costs about another $50. So on a story in Ottawa or Toronto, our direct cost is about $100.

On the other hand, Dale Goldhawk shot a story in Germany in 1977 – the aftermath of a hijacking – on that same 400-foot roll. But by the time we had flown him and his crew to Frankfurt (the camera gear costs about as much in excess baggage charges as another fare), had shot, processed and edited the film in Germany, and had satellited the story back to Toronto in time for the 6:00 newscast, the story had cost us $11,000, and would probably have cost us $15,000 in 1979. However, in the cost accounting of Cunningham's "smoke and mirrors," it was worth every last Deutschmark. We caught the story just as it crested, were in and out quickly without massive expenditures, and it gave the news service an international panache, which long outlasted the newscasts on which the items appeared.

Earlier I mentioned the CP 16, a 16-millimetre sound-on-film motion picture camera, still the basic picture unit for Global News, although we've moved strongly into ENG (electronic news gathering) at the Ottawa bureau. A CP 16 and the appropriate gear− tripod, lights, etc. − cost in excess of $20,000, and a cameraman can easily tie up another $5,000 in additional equipment. The ENG mini-cam, which transmits live pictures electronically, like the cameras in a TV studio, is even more expensive. RCA's TK76 B, with a portable VTR recorder and appropriate gear, costs about $80,000. The new Sony camera, with a lightweight Model 50 recorder and the requisite gear, would cost about $75,000. When you bear in mind the fact that a TV reporter is helpless without a camera crew and a camera, which he will probably tie up a full day in the pursuit of one story, you get some idea of the kind of financial commitment that must be made to get news on the air.

And it doesn't end there, of course. The best story ever shot is worthless until it can be delivered to the studio. In Canada, you can ship film or tape by air for a negligible amount of money, no more perhaps than you have tied up in the film. But to be competitive on a breaking story, you have to "feed" it by microwave or satellite. Unless you buy a permanent line from western Canada, for example, a single feed from Winnipeg costs $2,000 for ten minutes, the shortest time unit you can buy. A feed from Vancouver costs about twice that. Late in 1978, Global did buy a permanent western line, to feed programs to and get items from the member stations on our western news circuit − CKVU Vancouver, CFAC Calgary, CITV Edmonton, and CKND Winnipeg. But there is still a per-occasion charge for feeding items from the West to

Toronto, more than $500, which contributes to what can become a pretty grim total by the end of the month.

Ironically, it is often cheaper to get a story out of Europe or the Middle East than it is out of the Maritimes or B.C., a fact which tends to make nonsense of the politicians' lip service to national unity. I was in Israel and Lebanon in the spring of 1978, covering the Israeli incursion and the arrival of the hapless UN force. Because we were able to come to an arrangement with one of the U.S. networks (they were free to lift any visuals they needed from Global's footage) we were able to satellite daily reports to Toronto for about $700 per story, about a sixth of what it would have cost us at that time to feed from Vancouver. Even so, I had only five working days in Lebanon – five stories – and our costs were about $17,000, or about $3,400 per story.

When you compare our costs to those of the newspapers, their advantage becomes obvious. My Global colleague, Rae Corelli, spent a month in the Middle East in 1973, covering the Arab-Israeli war for the *Toronto Star*. He filed a dozen major stories in that time, and his expenses were $3,800. Even if you add $1,900 for converting 1973 money to 1978 money, the *Star*'s bill works out to about $475 a story, a seventh of Global's expenses in the same area.

There are times I have been in the middle of a story when I long to be in newspapers again. Television is so cumbersome, despite the fact that it looks so simple. We stoke up the smoke pots and we dazzle you with mirrors. We break our necks to make things look easy. But so many things can go wrong between getting the germ of an idea and a finished story on the air that I am constantly amazed when things work out the way we plan them.

Take the last days of South Vietnam, for example, when field producer John Scully, cameraman Wally Corbett, and I, were trying to film what was left of the war and the Army of the Republic of Vietnam's response to the last push by the North.

In the first place, the Vietnamese military briefing system was in ruins. The army of South Vietnam didn't know who was still fighting or where. So in the mornings, armed with a fistful of passes to the military districts where there might be resistance, we would head north, looking for a fire fight. Once we cooled our heels in jail for an hour for trying to cover the war with the wrong piece of paper.

On the days when we were lucky enough to find active resistance, shoot the story and get out unscathed, the real trouble was just beginning. Scully would do a quick shot list – the order and approximate length of the shots he felt would make a story – and then, in the heat and the confusion, as the car bounced back to Saigon, I would write my script. I would voice it on the lawn outside the Reuters office, our shipping point. As I recall, a complete film, packaged and labelled, had to be in the hands of the shipper by 2:00 P.M.

The shipper put it on a flight to Hong Kong, where, if things went well, the film was delivered to Viz News, where it was processed and cut, according to our enclosed instructions, in time for the evening ''bird'' – the satellite feed from Hong Kong to the U.S.

At least that's what happened if we hadn't had some problem with the camera and sound gear that we couldn't be aware of in the field, if the shipper got the film on the right flight, if the airline didn't manage to lose it in transit, if it cleared Hong Kong customs without too much delay, if the man responsible for making the delivery to Viz News didn't stop for a pot of tea, if the lab used by Viz News processed it properly, if the Viz News editor who cut the film understood our instructions and wasn't by nature and training an unfeeling butcher.

And if the film made it safely through all those stages, we had to hope that it wasn't squeezed off the satellite feed by the big networks, that the ''bird'' was relaying a clean picture, that the VTR operator in the States recorded it properly, and that it was transmitted safely to Toronto in time for the 6:00 news.

Once the story was safely on tape in Toronto, it was still subject to the daily obstacle course posed by the newscast itself, which I described earlier. What is astonishing is that most of the time it works. On that particular assignment, film we had shot in Vietnam in the morning on the death throes of an Asian nation was on the air in Toronto by 6:00 P.M. of the same calendar day. We missed only once in the two weeks we were there, and that was because, while the film was in the air between Saigon and Hong Kong, the story was overtaken by events. It became outdated, so it was not cut or fed. But the success rate is what keeps you in the business in the end. The daily miracle keeps on recurring.

As time goes on, the technology will get more and more foolproof. Before long, the sequence of events I have just described will sound to us like the early days of photography, when the cameraman had to squeeze a bulb and ignite a tray of flash powder, praying grimly that it wouldn't blow up in his face.

As a matter of fact, with the advent of ENG, what I have said about news film is already somewhat archaic. At the moment, most of us in Canada are using the mini-cam strictly as a portable recording device. Even used that way, the older models eliminate some problems almost immediately. The older, heavier recording units afford the news crew instant playback. If a shot doesn't work, you can do it again. It eliminates processing, another stage at which things can sometimes go wrong. The story can be edited rapidly on a VTR machine back at the studio, and when you put the item to air, it's on tape, always safer than film.

But the ENG concept goes far beyond its current use in Canada. Eventually, ENG gear will be accompanied by a compact transmission van with a disc on the roof. This will allow a news team to beam pictures back to the station, live into the newscast if there is some pressing editorial reason for doing it that way. And that will eliminate some additional problems. Because the field crew will be able to deal directly with the home station, it will have the effect of securing the transmission. The crew won't have to depend on a variety of disinterested operators, out of their control, who have the potential for messing things up at a number of points in the relay. ENG is already being used with the transmission van in the United States.

I was in New York briefly in the summer of 1977, when the city was being threatened by a hurricane, then sweeping north up the eastern seaboard. It was expected to hit New York about 8:00 P.M., and so ENG units for the early New York newscasts were sent south into the eye of the storm. They enabled reporters to stand in the middle of a wind- and water-torn landscape and report live into the newscasts. They were able to tell the viewers that this is exactly what the storm would look like when it reached New York two hours hence. It was very effective, and of valuable assistance for the authorities, who might otherwise have had some difficulty in persuading blasé New Yorkers to batten down the hatches. And it occurred to me that, for the first time, television news was becoming almost as easy as it had always appeared to be.

But some of us have serious misgivings about ENG, without wanting to tangle with the juggernaut of progess. Larry Stout of the CBC first raised doubts in my mind about ENG when he pointed out that it would cut deeply into the already limited ''think time'' of the reporter.

At the moment, the television reporter has two periods of relative calm in which to collect this thoughts, analyze the material he has gathered, probe his story line for weaknesses, isolate impressions that he can't completely substantiate, and write the script. One of these periods is in the cameraman's car or the plane, on the way back to the lab from the assignment. The second period is while the film is in the lab – thirty minutes to an hour, roughly, depending on the willingness of the lab and the amount of film that must be processed. When the film comes out of the lab, he must have recorded his voice track and be prepared to sit shoulder to shoulder with the editor, another vital team member, pulling the clips and the shots he needs to cover his report. Even now, this part of the journalistic process takes place on the run and ends in a dead heat with the film editor.

But what happens to the reporter when he has no travel time back to the studio, because the material will be transmitted from the van, and when he has no lab time, because tape requires no processing? When, after he has assembled his facts, will he have time to think about them, to weigh what he wants to say? It will be the newspaper equivalent of writing running copy, that is, writing the story, paragraph by paragraph, as it unfolds. Newspaper reporters have to do that when a deadline intervenes before the story has come to a natural conclusion. It rarely produces great journalism, even when allowances are made for the circumstances.

What also worries me about the pressure of ENG is that it may put an undue emphasis on cool performance rather than on thoughtful journalism. It may begin to produce a series of glib, quick-draw artists rather than steady and responsible sharp-shooters, like the best reporters now. That would be a development that TV news, already plagued by honeyed tones and pretty faces, could ill afford.

And there is another problem that may be heightened by ENG. Even now, the TV camera tends to become part of the story. We have all heard about the peaceful demonstration that suddenly becomes vocal and violent simply because a TV camera has arrived on the scene. I myself have watched lounging strikers leap to their feet and begin picketing furiously when a news team arrived on the story – a fact I was always careful to report.

But the camera's intervention can be more insidious than that. I remember covering an Ontario Hydro strike in Toronto in the early seventies. When I arrived with a camera crew, it was fairly quiet on the picket line outside Hydro's Bloor Street offices, and it stayed that way.

We didn't have much to film until one of the union organizers remembered that it was pay day. Although the strikers had been out for several days, there was money owing to them from earlier in the pay period, and the organizers decided to ask for it. We asked permission to go with them to the personnel department, and they gladly gave it to us.

We went up in the elevator in a group, the camera rolling. We threaded our way through the islands of plants and desks in one of those open floor plans to a corner cubicle where an unsuspecting supervisor was waiting: the trade unionists first, then the cameraman, still rolling, and me, clutching a microphone, bringing up the rear.

To my astonishment, when we walked in on the supervisor, unannounced, he played the game. He pretended the camera wasn't there, as if he were an actor in a television play. He didn't even glance in our direction. He chatted with the organizers in a normal tone of voice, ascertained what they wanted, and then telephoned his boss for a decision. He hung up finally, and there was a lull. We shut off the camera, and he recognized our presence then. I think he asked us all if we wanted a cup of coffee.

Then came the word that his boss, one of the company's senior officials, would be pleased to meet the union somewhere else. Again we tagged along, unchallenged, with the camera rolling.

The senior official dealt with the camera in exactly the same way the supervisor had. He ignored it. They talked back and forth for a time, the union organizers and the executive, each side taking a position.

Finally they came to an impasse, and there was a pregnant pause in the conversation. Their every vibration seemed to beg intervention, a word from the chair. And then suddenly, astoundingly, I heard myself mediating. Asking questions, yes. But mediating.

"Mr. Executive, this gentleman says such and such. Now if he were willing to do so and so, would that be agreeable to you?"

I continued in that vein, probing at the position of one side and then the other, until the answer was obvious. And as quickly as it began, it was settled.

What worried me later when I thought about it, and what continues to worry me now, is that all of us, the management people, the union organizers, the impartial reporter, were for a time prisoners of television. As a result of our long hours in front of television sets, each of us played, without prompting, what we knew to be appropriate roles.

Only an insensitive clod could work in television and not be worried about where it is taking us.

CHAPTER EIGHT

The Politicians and the Critics

In the terminology of space, there is "the window" – a precise point above the earth in space and time through which a rocket must be fired if it is to assume the right course and trajectory to carry out its assigned mission. And for politicians, there is a window in TV news coverage, the precise, attention-grabbing statement, delivered at precisely the right time, that is so much to the point of the reporter's story that he can't afford to assemble his film without it.

Some Canadian politicians recognize the existence of the window, and have trained themselves to hit it with reasonable frequency. Others know it's there, but miss consistently, usually because they don't know how to end a sentence or when to end one, because what they say is unorganized or badly put, or because they haven't been able to isolate either the point of the debate or the central issue of the story they're trying to be part of. They do not script themselves, or rehearse, but instead rely on their wits, a practice that is more dangerous for some than others. No television pro would take that risk.

For some reason or other, the existence of such a window causes resentment. I was talking about it to a group of lawyers not so long ago. I had been invited to speak after a well-known Toronto legal firm's annual dinner, and in the cross-examination that followed my prepared talk I was taken to task for daring to admit that such a window existed. Why should politicians be required to clamber through a window or anything else of TV's making, one lawyer wanted to know. I could only point out that the window was there, freely available to anyone with the wit and talent to use it.

Surely this is not the only skill a politician requires if he is to be successful in public life. He accepts the fact that he must learn to use a public platform, to speak robustly and loquaciously, to think on his feet. As a matter of fact, in the Canadian House of Commons it is considered bad form to speak from a prepared text in the course of a debate. In the mother of Parliaments, Westminster, only ministers and opposition front-benchers may read their speeches. And if you want to be successful nationally in this country, you must learn the other official language, at least to the point of being able to read it.

Added to that now is the necessity for being able to use the new medium. Politicians had to learn the basics of television very early. They soon found out that they were not to grab the microphone, for example, and to look at the man asking the questions, because turning to the camera made them look *gauche* and too eager. The politicians had to learn to speak at a reasonable speed, because speaking too slowly was deadly dull, and speaking too quickly obscured the message and gave the impression he was too hyper to be trusted.

Robert Kennedy had a problem with television, which he never overcame. He spoke awkwardly and he knew it, so he talked quickly. He found it difficult to hit the target with a single word or phrase, so he spewed them rapidly, a shot-gun approach. He may have obliterated the target, but his audience could never be sure.

As John Whale points out in *The Half-Shut Eye*, American producers feel that about two words a second is a good delivery rate for the commentary on a documentary film. In the U.K. and Canada, broadcasters tend to speak a little faster, but they believe that about three words a second is just about the limit. (I myself speak somewhere between two and a half and three words a second, depending, I find, on the circumstances and the story.) Robert Kennedy, however, regularly rattled along at three and a half words a second, and sometimes hit four.

Is it somehow demeaning that politicians should have to learn these things? Is it manipulative of them to study the medium and try to meet its immutable requirements? I can't see that it is. The window concept is just a little more sophisticated, and the politicians who understand it are grateful that it exists.

Stewart Smith, the Ontario leader of the Liberal Party, once told me that despite its faults, television news remains the best way of getting through to his constituency. In the newspapers, you often have three strikes against you before you begin. But in the fifteen or thirty-second news clip you are at last on your own. It doesn't matter how trivial, inept, or even vindictive the reporter is, or how inaccurate his script. The politician still has a chance to clamber through the window and reach the voters.

President Kennedy was one of the first political masters of the medium. He not only learned how to speak for television, he learned how to cater to its demand for theatre. President Kennedy saw foreign trips as an obvious political opportunity, a truth that has not been lost on successive Presidents and Canadian Prime Ministers. To a large extent, a foreign trip is the kind of scenario that is subject to reasonable political control. The principal is able to choose the reason for the trip, in effect to set the stage. He chooses the set and the cast of characters. And when reporters set foot on foreign soil, they tend to suspend their critical faculties in a way that does not happen at home. The foreign trip is also fertile ground for those non-news events that so enliven our political campaigns these days, the so-called "photo opportunities."

In the whistle-stop days of North American politics, before television and before the advent of the press plane, particularly as an election campaign drew to a close, the candidates made a point of "going where the ducks are." What that meant really, was going somewhere where the candidate had a chance to bag a few votes. There was no point wasting time in an area of the constituency that was already lost or already safe. The candidate went where his presence might be expected to count, where he could hope to tip the balance in his favour.

But in recent years, it hasn't been nearly so much the political geography that determines where a leader goes. He doesn't worry half as much as he used to about a handful of votes in any one place, because television has become the real constituency. Pierre Trudeau, for example, kicked off his 1979 election campaign in

Earlton, a small Ontario town near North Bay. For Trudeau, there were no ducks in Earlton. The riding was a safe NDP constituency, Temiskaming, although a bright young Liberal candidate did run strongly there. Where the ducks were, for the Prime Minister, was in Toronto, where he didn't even set up a blind until a few days later.

The Prime Minister's staff chose Earlton for the opener for a number of reasons. A Prime Minister had never visited Earlton before, and might never again, so there was theatre in it for one thing. It was a considerable local event that might be expected to attract a large number of properly impressed people. The community has the right French-English mixture for a country torn by cultural differences. French and English signs on Earlton's store fronts would make useful television symbolism. Since Earlton was a small town, the Prime Minister's going there at the start gave the impression that he was plunging quickly into the grassroots, among ordinary people. And the visit was timed so that it would be on the TV screens in Toronto, and hence the rest of the country, that evening.

The campaign as a whole went the same way. In a moment of off-the-record candour, one of the NDP's backroom boys told the *Globe and Mail*: "Campaigning is now almost entirely devoted to producing a television show." The advance men are alert for "photo opportunities."

In such a campaign, clearly, the emphasis shifts from complex matters of policy to simple, flashy promises that are more likely to be readily understood by the voters than kept. The new goals determine the candidate's daily schedule. The planners try to provide something visual for television in the mornings, so that the TV news crews have time to cut and feed their items for the early newscasts; something with a little more meat in it in the afternoon, with words and ideas for the newspapers, but not entirely devoid of visual interest, because the network will probably want to feed an updated version of their early reports for the late news.

The candidates must have television news time because they know it will reach, at least in a subliminal way, the people who often decide elections, the people who aren't really interested.

What that meant in 1979 was putting Trudeau into crowd scenes as often as possible (praying only that no one heckled him about Margaret) to give the impression that the Trudeaumania of a decade before still lived. It meant keeping Joe Clark out of too many situations that he might not be able to control, so that he always looked strong and capable to the people who doubted whether he had the stuff of leadership. It meant putting Ed Broadbent into homes and factories, getting him to barbecues and fairs, to enhance his image as a man of the people.

Merely to stick one's candidate into the public eye, particularly if there is any doubt that he can walk and chew gum at the same time, isn't enough, however. The danger is not so much that he will change people's minds by tumbling down the steps from an airplane, like Gerald Ford, or fumbling a football like Robert Stanfield, or stepping briskly into a bayonet like Joe Clark, the most recent addition to the awkward squad. The danger is that he will get caught up in some kind of visual vignette that dramatizes what people have suspected about him all along. Of course the less people know of the candidates and their policies, the more likely such trifles are to survive as vivid personal symbolism.

But too much credit is given to television as an instrument for changing people's political convictions. For one thing, the audience is much more astute than either the political organizers or many television producers seem to realize.

Since the first Great Debate – Kennedy vs Nixon in 1960 – the analysts have concluded that such confrontations tend to crystallize attitudes rather than alter them. Like the Canadian debate in the 1979 election, they tend to reinforce the status quo.

I think the same thing can be said of political advertising during an election campaign. I went to Perth, Ontario, a town of about 5,000 in the Tory heartland of Lanark County, as the 1979 campaign was drawing to a close. I wanted to do a man-on-the-street survey on the effects of the three parties' advertising blitz. It was hardly a scientific sample, but I think it's significant that out of the twenty people we had on camera, only one was ready to admit that political advertising had ever changed her vote.

My own mail over the years has reinforced my doubt about television's political influence. People tend to read into things whatever they want to. Sometimes, on a single news item, we have had letters from the supporters of each of the three major parties, each of them claiming that we were unfair to the candidate they supported. As a matter of fact, I have come to regard the mail as a litmus test of political impartiality. If the supporters of all three major parties complain, I suspect that we're doing a pretty fair job.

One of the most dramatic pieces of campaign propaganda ever published was a simple Democratic poster in 1960. It featured a truly awful picture of Richard Nixon, five-o'clock shadow, eyes that seemed to avoid the viewers, "Tricky Dick" at his worst. At the bottom of the poster was a single devastating question: "Would you buy a used car from this man?" Most of America, as it turned out, wouldn't. But the truth is that the poster had major impact only on those who thought Nixon looked shifty in the first place. People who tended to favour Nixon either didn't understand it at all, or saw it only as evidence of the depths to which the Democrats would stoop.

It would be dishonest to pretend that the attitudes of individual newsmen towards particular politicians have no effect on coverage. They do, particularly when it comes to an assessment of how the candidate is likely to fare at a convention or at the polls. The three Canadian networks pay very little attention to the candidates of the extreme right and the extreme left, not because no newsmen have sympathy for them, but because they're convinced that they can't possibly win.

The same thing happens at political conventions. When the Tories chose the unknown westerner who was to become Prime Minister, Global had very little money to spend. We couldn't compete with the continuous live coverage of the CBC and CTV, so we decided to gamble. We committed all our resources to a half-hour profile on the most attractive candidate, at least on film, Brian Mulroney. The Tory convention didn't share Global's judgement and so the half-hour profile that was going to reward our political acumen turned out to be the half-hour profile on the most spectacular loser. We comforted ourselves with the notion that we were living up to Global's promise of performance to the CRTC for "alternative" programming.

Some weeks before the convention, I had a call at the anchor desk from some ebullient young man touting Joe Clark as a candidate. He was, he said, part of Clark's Toronto "organization." I wasn't rude enough to laugh in his face, but I wasn't very polite either. I made it clear that I didn't think Clark was a serious contender, and that I could see no point in sending a Global reporter to meet him.

My view of Clark was coloured by what I remembered of him during the Diefenbaker campaign of 1965. He was attached to the Chief's doting entourage as a representative of the Young Progressive Conservatives. I found him collegiate, callow and pompous beyond his years and I wasn't impressed. If, in retrospect, I appear to be at least as pompous as I thought Clark to be, it wasn't necessarily because I was wrong about him, but because I thought he couldn't win.

Clark's people viewed the media coverage of his ill-fated pre-election swing around the world as proof that we were out to get him. I admit that I too had some misgivings about the coverage as I watched satellite reports, night after night, from my colleague Rae Corelli. They dealt with Clark's lacklustre performance in Japan, the lost baggage in Bangkok, the awkward moments in India, and finally, Clark's comic opera procession out of Jerusalem behind a garbage truck. But I talked to Corelli when he got back to Toronto, spoke of my misgivings about the coverage, and came away convinced that he'd treated Clark not only with scrupulous objectivity, but with considerable mercy. The real trip was several degrees worse.

This is not to say that politicians are never, at times, the victims of bias, pack-reporting, and stupefying incompetence. But it is trivial-mindedness rather than bloody-mindedness on the part of the media that thoughtful politicians fear most.

At a recent California conference on "docu-dramas" like "Roots" and "Holocaust," columnist Art Buchwald sat fidgeting while network news executives and critics complained one after the other that such spectacles were endangering the credibility of serious news programs. Finally, Buchwald could stand it no longer. He asked what made them think that the evening newscasts and the news magazine programs were not also docu-dramas.

"I've been at congressional hearings that lasted for four hours," he said, "and on the news they use only the one tiny snippet where the Senator screams at the witness, 'You are a blaggart and a liar, sir.' Is that an accurate picture of what went on there?"

I don't think that Buchwald was suggesting that the whole four-hour hearing should have been carried on television. But he was urging television news to resist the temptation to carry only the juicy bits and to try instead to concentrate on the issues.

Even when a news item isolates the serious points of the debate, however, it can be turned into a carnival by the editing technique. "Intercutting" two separate political interviews, that is, using a quote from one interview followed by a countering quote from another, can often create what John Whale describes as "a bizarre dialogue of the deaf." Without the questions, or some other form of reportorial bridge, the two interviewees seem to be ploughing blithely on as if the other hadn't spoken. Indeed, at the time of the interview, the other man was not within earshot. Use of this technique is usually well-intentioned, but unless the people being interviewed are speaking precisely to the same points, it distorts. And in any event it means that through the magic of television, a debate is being created which never took place.

It is also true that the reporter's attempt to bring political balance to a story can distort. On the surface, it might appear that to use three pertinent fifteen-second clips from each of the party leaders in the day's story on the debate in the House would ensure even-handed reporting. It can, but only if the facts themselves are in some kind of balance. If the government is taking a fearful licking from the opposition in the Commons, strictly on debating points, it is not even-handed to pick the best fifteen-second clip by the Prime Minister and lump it in with two of a number of telling comments from the leaders of the opposition parties. Such a story is seriously imbalanced, in the government's favour.

There are also pitfalls of omission. Not the least gaping of these comes about because in almost any interview situation the politician is in a combative position. He wants to leave the impression that his position is the only right one. For the sake of balance, not to mention his own self-respect, the reporter, in his interview or in the script, must make it clear that the politician's position is only one of several.

The serious viewer should also keep it in mind that the politicians are firmly in control of what news will be filmed or taped for television and what news won't. It is almost an axiom of North American politics that the cameras must never be allowed to cover any meaningful part of the political process. They are there only for the colour, the staged events, the conventions, and sometimes the debates. Understandably, cameras are not allowed into caucus meetings or cabinet meetings, and they are not always welcome at the conferences between federal and provincial leaders.

It is only recently that cameras have been allowed into the House of Commons. And they are not CBC, or CTV or Global cameras, but parliamentary cameras, under the same austere control as Hansard, the official printed record. We are fortunate in this country, thanks to cable television, that there are channels available to carry what for many people is dull, unrewarding programming. If the standards of television, rather than those of Hansard (which reports oaths and Bronx cheers as "Some Hon. Members – Hear, hear") were allowed to dictate Commons coverage, it would make much better viewing. At the moment, however, the Commons cameras wear blinders. There are no shots of members reacting to a telling point in a speech. The camera remains glued to the speaker. If someone storms out in a hot debate, his exit is ignored.

But far be it for a television newsman to look a gift horse in the mouth. It has at least saved us, the politicians and the viewers, from the nightly scrum, in which a mob of newsmen, waving a forest of notebooks and microphones, used to buttonhole the key figures outside the House when the debate was over. Before debates were televised, and clips from them were freely available, it was the only way to get the principals on film.

The politicians' fears about the wisdom of televising debates in the House have proved at least to some extent to be unfounded. What terrified them before the decision was taken was that the cameras would reveal widespread absenteeism, and that some of their number would be inclined to mug a bit for the audience. As usual, they underestimated the public, which soon demonstrated that it was perfectly capable of understanding that a member's business would not allow him to attend every sitting. What MPs hadn't counted on was that the public would see Canada's finest private club for what it was, that most people would be capable of distinguishing between good and bad debate, between the schoolboy antics of the question period and truly penetrating inquiries, between awkward attempts at humour and real wit. And if televising the debates in the Commons doesn't have the effect of raising the public's standards about the kind of men it will elect, then it isn't just television which will have failed, but the parliamentary system.

A politician or anyone else doing television in a studio setting has to begin with a deception. The deception may be abandoned in time, as cameras become more light sensitive, but at the moment, the candlepower needed to illuminate a set makes human flesh, even healthy human flesh, look white and sickly. In addition, the heat of the lights causes perspiration and facial shininess.

Since no politician wants to look sick or nervous, he can't very well go on the air without make-up and powder. But most politicians are not anxious to have it known that they're wearing it, for fear that it would erode their machismo. As a result, very early on, U.S. networks like CBS had an iron-clad rule that no photographers would be allowed into make-up rooms where politicians were being prettied up for the air. Women politicians don't have the image problem, of course, but even they need heavier make-up for television than they may be accustomed to wearing.

I recall an interview that Peter Desbarats and I did with Prime Minister Trudeau just before the Quebec election that gave us Premier Lévesque. The mobile was set up in the street, outside Trudeau's office in the Langevin block. The office itself was cluttered with cables, cameras, lights, and technicians, and the crew was working against the clock to get ready.

Prime Minister Trudeau arrived on time and he was clearly impatient about the delay. While he waited in a temporary cubicle outside the office door, a make-up lady worked on his face. We'd hired a still photographer to do some publicity work and the Prime Minister must have spotted him out of the corner of his eye.

To my surprise, just before the interview began, he made an issue of it. He was polite but firm. Any pictures taken while he was being made-up would have to be destroyed. He was holding Desbarats personally responsible and if a picture eventually appeared anywhere, there would be an unspecified kind of hell to pay. It was, in my view, just another instance of a politician underestimating his constituency and worrying about the wrong images.

I think one of the things that hurt Trudeau the most in 1979 had nothing to do with the campaign, little to do with the man himself (unless you blame him for the original error) and little to do with how it was presented on television. I mean Margaret's defection.

Unlike many of my peers, I do not believe that the antics of Mrs. Trudeau were forgotten or forgiven by the Canadian electorate. Margaret was the first big chink in Trudeau's armour, the first indication that he might be flawed, both as a man and a leader. I don't think sympathy translates into votes. Sympathy is for losers.

And yet Trudeau handled the Margaret crisis flawlessly, at least at his periodic news conferences, when he was ready for the questions. But his campaign managers were terrified about the Margaret issue while he was on the hustings, not because of what the raising of the issue might do to voters' attitudes but because of what it did to Trudeau's attitude each time it cropped up unexpectedly. They had seen the Prime Minister explode in that icy, controlled way of his at an early meeting in Vancouver. And what appeared on the newscasts was not so much the original heckling (someone called out something nasty about his wife) but the cold, tough, hostile Trudeau the incident created, a Trudeau who savaged his audience and ultimately the viewers from that moment on.

Earlier, in an interview that Peter Desbarats and I did with the Prime Minister at the start of the campaign, he had used the

Margaret question to his own advantage. Before the taping began, Peter and I had discussed the rumours that a reconciliation was imminent and decided that one of us had to ask him about it. To my great relief, it was agreed that Desbarats would ask the question. It was the wrong decision.

When Desbarats popped the question deep into the interview, Trudeau rounded on him and asked Peter about his own marriage, which had just recently gone on the rocks.

"What about it, Peter?" the Prime Minister asked. "Is there any chance of reconciliation in your marriage?"

Desbarats was ready and willing to do battle, on obvious grounds, and did for a time until I interrupted the unproductive sparring and changed the subject.

For all politicians, Trudeau's defeat in 1979 must raise questions about how best to deal with the media. In the beginning, newsmen and voters alike were entranced by his willingness to manhandle sacred cows in the open, to react in a human way to stupid or impertinent questions, to utter obvious truths that few members of the establishment had dared to advertise before him. He was at ease in front of the cameras. He felt free to clown in front of them and to reveal his disdain for the people behind them. But by 1979, Mr. Trudeau's frankness seemed to have worn out its welcome.

In the mid-sixties, one of the most attractive figures in British politics was Jo Grimond, the leader of the ever-hopeful Liberal Party. Like Trudeau, he was very much himself on television, and like Trudeau he acknowledged in so many words that some aspects of politics were mindless and unreasonable.

In 1968, Senator Eugene McCarthy, trying to nail down the Democratic nomination for the presidency, exhibited the same kind of quality. He seemed to be totally unself-conscious on television, perhaps because it never occurred to him that he could fail to convince thoughtful people of the justice of his positions on key issues. In contrast, people like Hubert Humphrey and Richard Nixon were "up" instantly when the camera lights winked on. Unlike McCarthy, they seemed more concerned with managing other people's points of view than explaining their own. The contrast seemed to ensure the undying support of McCarthy's followers, but it somehow failed to appeal to a sufficiently large number of American voters.

When you consider Trudeau's defeat in 1979, Grimond's lack of success as the leader of the British Liberals, and McCarthy's failure in the United States, you begin to suspect that ease, honesty, and forthright behaviour in front of the cameras may not be the best qualities for an aspiring politician. It may simply be that if a politician is too confident and too smooth on television, the public sees him in the same light as it sees the charmers who sell us beer and razor blades. It begins to wonder about his motives.

One of the first things that a politician must decide in his relations with the media is whether he wants to score debating points off the people asking the questions, the journalists, or whether he wants to get through to the viewers, listeners, and readers. Prime Minister Trudeau never seemed to know whether he wanted to devastate the reporters or reach the audience beyond them. When he gave in to his considerable temper, and that magnificent face froze, it not only frightened reporters but viewers as well. Press relations and public relations were out the window in one stroke.

There is a very thin line between suffering fools gladly and exhibiting a little spine. Nixon tended to fall off the other side of the horse. You could ask Nixon the most insulting questions, and he would reply in honeyed tones that he was "not a crook." If he had revealed a little honest anger when he was asked that sort of question, it would have lent credibility to his reply. A man who smiles and replies reasonably when you ask him how much he'd charge for murdering his grandmother, is not to be trusted.

On the other hand, you can't rule out dedicated sycophancy as a way of getting at the media either. Knowing what a correspondent or an anchorman has said recently on the air, and commenting favourably on it, is good for their uncertain egos and it may pay off in improved relations. No one is more open to flattery than what is known as the on-air personality.

But Paul Godfrey, now the chairman of Metropolitan Toronto, implanted himself firmly in the public eye by using another ploy in his media relations – "producerism." When he was a mere controller in the Borough of North York, Godfrey kept in touch not so much with the obvious contacts, the reporters, but with the assignment desks, the real fount of decision-making. If Paul Godfrey went to give a speech on mill rates or cut the ribbon at an old folks' home, he called the city's assignment editors first, personally. During one period, when I was on the Toronto regional assignment desk for the CBC, Godfrey called as often as once a day.

If the TV newsmen are the most prominent members of a government's unofficial opposition, the politicians are the unofficial critics when it comes to television news. Often they are better informed than the real critics, the motley crew that gossips about the industry on the entertainment pages of the daily newspapers.

Shortly after I left the CBC the first time, I was negotiating with the *Toronto Star* for a job as a national reporter based in Toronto. I've forgotten whether the *Star* approached me, or I approached the *Star*. But at some point in our discussions, knowing that their regular TV columnist had just quit, I mentioned to the editor I was dealing with that perhaps it was just about time they hired someone to write a television column who knew something about the subject. I made it clear that I was interested.

"Oh hell," came the reply. "What would you want to do that for when you could have a real job on the paper?"

Unfortunately, that has been the traditional newspaper attitude towards TV criticism and the entertainment pages generally.

I remember as a very junior reporter on the *Ottawa Journal* being asked to review a play on my night off. I had no particular interest in the stage or any experience as a critic, which I am sure was clear enough in the subsequent review. And the *Journal*'s record in the area of television criticism at that time was even worse. The *Journal* had refused to recognize television for some time, in the apparent belief that if they ignored it long enough it would go away. The *Journal* did not believe in reminding people of either the electronic or the print competition. One could not in the columns of the *Journal* refer to a resident as an "Ottawa citizen," since that also happened to be the name of the afternoon paper down the street.

Then as now, at least in the Toronto production centre, too many television columnists don't know their business, a direct result of the newspapers' failure to take television seriously. The same newspapers, which would never dream of assigning someone to Parliament Hill who didn't know Canadian politics, or someone to Quebec who didn't speak French, think nothing of hiring a television columnist who doesn't know the difference between film and tape. They do, however, know what they like, or, more to the point, what they don't like. And they have the ability to say it in a clever and often sadistic way. That seems to be one of the job specifications. This is too bad, because there has never been a period when television required intelligent criticism and informed reporting more than the present. There are some good critics, but in my experience they are the exception rather than the rule.

The irony is that the television industry, or at least certain parts of it, worry about what the critics say. I don't know how it is now at the CBC, but in my time, the people who ran information programs danced attendance on them. I can remember a particularly painful session in Nash's office with a nasty young man who eventually deserted to the CRTC. He suspected, quite rightly, that Warren Davis wouldn't be allowed to do more than read as the new host of "The National," and Nash swallowed every insult.

I used to badger Nash to cut them off. Instead, there were press previews, advance screenings, and cocktail parties to launch performers. Nash himself used to go so far as to invite them into his own living room. For the CBC, the ink itself was more important than the quality or the accuracy of what was written. As long as the columnists got the channel and the time right, the corporation didn't seem to care.

Much of what passes for television criticism is mere gossip. It was reported in the spring of 1979 in one of the entertainment columns of the *Toronto Sun* that I was leaving Global to become the news vice-president at one of the stations in Vancouver. The columnist checked with the owner of the station, who told him it was untrue. The rumour and the denial were published anyway, perhaps only because the columnist needed to fill space. Needless to say, no one from the *Sun* telephoned me about the story. I suppose a second denial would have killed it completely. But rumours, once started, have lives of their own and I spent the next few months telling my friends that there was nothing to it.

Accuracy doesn't appear to be a primary consideration of the entertainment pages. If the Global newsroom had really been in the kind of straits described by an endless series of piddling little items in the columns, we'd have been off the air. It astounded me that a paper like the *Toronto Star*, which traditionally had had one of the unhappiest newsrooms in the country, would even contemplate printing a story about the low morale at Global or anywhere else.

But then the newspapers' criticism of television has always revealed a double standard. The *Toronto Sun*, whose columnists, with the exception of Bob Pennington, have been foul to Global, and lofty about the wastelands of commercial television, really throw stones. If, like a network's audience, the *Sun*'s readership fluctuated by thousands every week, it might be even more grunt-oriented than it is now. It is one of the anomalies of broadcasting that its chief competitor is also its chief critic.

I have often thought that somewhere in a news hour, along with business and sports, there might be room for a review of the papers, a critical analysis of the press along the lines of the newspaper criticism of television. But I have long since concluded that such a segment would not have much popular appeal. If people really cared about the quality of the newspapers, they'd be a great deal better.

What upsets me most, however, about the unofficial criticism of the politicians and the official criticism of the newspapers, is not what they have said, but what they haven't.

As a television anchorman, I used to console myself with the belief that if we weren't giving people enough information on which to base intelligent decisions about their lives and their country, we were at least stimulating them to seek additional information from books, magazines, and newspapers. I am no longer sure how successful we are in arousing their active curiosity. Television has become firmly entrenched as the average Canadian's primary source of news.

And I am less sure that prodding them towards the newspapers would serve much useful purpose. In meeting the challenge of television, the newspapers have begun to ape it. Television is essentially episodic, and nowhere is that more apparent than in a TV newscast. The judgement of the industry, as expressed in television newscasts, is that the attention span of the average North American is somewhere between a minute and thirty seconds and two minutes. That is the length of the average visual item, the average story. Similarly, a producer who is putting together a half-hour documentary may at some point break it into sequences. If he hasn't got enough film to sustain a dozen two-minute sequences, he hasn't got a half hour. The slick American television drama is structured in much the same way, from jolt to jolt.

I am convinced that it isn't just television's content that is having an influence on the audience, but its form. And television's form is being imposed not just on the general audience, but on the people who own and market newspapers. The *Toronto Star* is becoming more and more like a television newscast. The headlines are bigger, the pictures bolder, the stories fewer and shorter. The *Star* wouldn't be doing it if it weren't selling papers. And I begin to suspect that television, which as an industry has set its sights on the lowest common denominator, has actually succeeded in shortening the average attention span.

Television is perhaps the most important single influence of our time. I have felt for years that the greatest threat to Canada's integrity as a nation is not the crisis in Quebec or the falling dollar, but American television. Think of the hours we and our children have spent in front of television sets, escaping. Think of the overwhelming preponderance of American programming, which in an unobtrusive way pumps us full of American values, American hopes, American history, even American patterns of speech. Never mind the Canadian flag, or Canadian pride or the July 1 extravaganzas on Parliament Hill. Will we, after another twenty or thirty years of the gentle insistence of American programming, have the will to survive as a nation? I don't see how.

What angers me, then, about the politicians' and the newspapers' approach to television is that they have largely ignored what television is doing to us. The Ontario government recently commissioned Judy LaMarsh to do a study of television violence, it's true. But there is a growing suspicion that it is the character of the medium rather than the program content which contributes most to violence.

Harry Boyle, a distinguished broadcaster and writer who spent ten years with the Canadian Radio and Television Commission (CRTC), the last couple of years as chairman, seems to be one of the few people in this country who is concerned about the scope of the television revolution.

In a talk to a church media group in Toronto, early in 1979, Boyle dwelt on the changes wrought by television. Citing Tony Schwartz's book, *The Responsive Chord,* Boyle pointed out that when Gutenberg invented the printing press, "man lived by a communications system requiring the laborious coding of thought into words, and then the equally laborious uncoding by the receiver, similar to the loading, shipping and unloading of a railway freight car.''

With television, the freight car has become a blurred mosaic of light and sound that must be stored and recalled at high speed. Communication is no longer a reflective process. With television, a communications barrier has been crossed, akin to the ninety-mile-an-hour barrier beyond which the motorcycle driver has to turn in rather than out to stay upright through a skid.

''In communicating with an audience at electronic speed,'' Boyle continued, ''we no longer direct information into an audience, but try to evoke stored information out of it, in a patterned sort of way. He [Schwartz] contends that 500 years of experience of patiently transmitting experience line by line, usually left to right, down the printed page, is no longer right.''

Boyle cited the printing press as one communications revolution, a revolution that brought with it a growing public perception of a right to information. By the nineteenth century, when the daily newspaper was commonplace on the European breakfast table, that right had become firmly entrenched. Radio was another revolutionary medium.

"When you say that," Boyle noted, "quite often you get a response from people who don't quite believe it. But think of what Roosevelt did with radio. Think of what Hitler did with radio: those loudspeakers in those corners of every German town back in the thirties. Think what Churchill did with radio. Think what de Gaulle did with radio."

Radio was also the thin edge of the wedge for entertainment. But because of people like Edward R. Murrow and Matthew Halton it has remained an effective instrument for pure information; it continued to service what the public perceived as its right to be informed.

"Now," said Boyle, "think of the television revolution. Think of the fight there is in this country about television. I know. I've been through it for ten years. The demand for American television stations in this country has nothing to do with the right to be informed. It is the right to be entertained, and that is inherent in it all."

Ironically, it was the CRTC's own decision to licence cable television in this country, which has ensured an even greater influx of American programming, and by fragmenting the marketplace for the Canadian commercial broadcaster, has made Canadian programming less and less competitive. With a smaller share of the advertising dollar, there is less money available for individual Canadian broadcasters to produce Canadian content.

Because of the competition of fragmentation, and the competition inherent in the nature of television itself, the producer is addressing his audience at the same level as he would address a group that has bought and paid for a seat at the movies. Not at all at the level he would address a group that has filed into a lecture hall, or the visitors' gallery in the House of Commons, or the pews of a church. "It is fundamentally the music hall," as Boyle puts it.

To hang onto the audience, to hold onto the ratings, the producer of a half-hour program must somehow entice an audience which the producer of the previous half hour assembled or held onto for another purpose. To do that, the emphasis must be on entertainment rather than information. Even the Russians, with their state-controlled television, have realized that basic truth, dictated not by political ideology, but by the implacable nature of the medium.

It is time for us to pause, to stop reaching for every new bit of technology like the *Toronto Star*'s much-vaunted fibre optics system, that will give us 150 chances to watch re-runs of ''Gilligan's Island'' instead of ten or twenty. It is time for us to take stock of what television has already done to us.

''When I fight with the Minister of Communications,'' Boyle said, ''I am not fighting so much about the technology as the fact that there are millions and millions of dollars being spent on researching technology and hardware and no money being spent at all on what it's going to do and what you want it for.''

It may be that it is the responsibility of the broadcasters themselves to fund research into the effects of television on the Canadian viewer. But that has never been the tradition in this country, and to prove it one has to look no further than the distillers and the brewers. Like the broadcasters, they produce the stuff, pump it out of the building, and to hell with the consequences to the unwary consumer.

But if the politicians, the Commons broadcasting committee, the CRTC, and the critics had been doing their jobs all this time, perhaps the broadcasters would have been forced to do something.

CHAPTER NINE

What's Wrong With TV News

Much of what is wrong with television news is also wrong with Canadian journalism as a whole. The people who own television stations and newspapers are not radically different. Whether they are actually members of the traditional Canadian establishment, or only knocking on the door, they exhibit little stomach for challenging the old order, or for meeting the new realities with new ideas.

And although Canadian television news is no longer in its infancy, it is still doing very little to train bright young people on its own. It is much easier to let them get some experience first on newspapers, and then teach them television skills after they have acquired a journalistic foundation in print. This is bad for at least two reasons. In the first place, it means that many of the people hired for television are already afflicted with all the ingrained wisdom of what is essentially a traditional medium with a constrictive set of disciplines; and in the second place, it means that too many people in television news have not had the opportunity to grow up with and develop an instinctive use of film.

Standards are much higher now than they were when I began a quarter of a century ago. Today, people like me would not only have trouble getting a job, they would have trouble getting through an editor's door. But the standards haven't risen quickly enough. They have not kept pace with the increasing complexity of our society, or, more important, with the rising educational standards, general knowledge, and sophistication of the people who make up that society. This doesn't mean simply that we aren't good enough. It means that we aim too low.

Although few of them would consider doing anything else, journalists have never had a very comfortable opinion of their own calling. Perhaps that's because they know more about their failings than anyone else. But even at a time when a Bachelor of Journalism degree is almost a prerequisite to employment, it is possible for Gerald Leblanc, the president of the Fédération professionnelle des journalistes du québec, the largest journalists' organization in the province, to say, in June of 1978, in an unequivocal way:

"Journalism is not a profession...with formal training, a definite code of practice, and permits; but is somewhere between a trade, an artistic endeavour and industrial work."

Although journalists have long since abandoned the fedora, the press card, and the hip flask as badges of office, there continue to be legacies from the Front Page era. And the worst of these is cynicism. Unfortunately, it is the most common attribute of most of the people who've spent any time in Canadian newsrooms; an abiding, sour, all-pervading cynicism about man and most of his works. If this meant simply that politicians and press agents and PR men were always suspect, it would be bad enough. But it also colours our coverage of issues.

Overpopulation, the Third World, refugees, the North-South dialogue, become a bore. Politicians' speeches, no matter what the content, become vastly enervating. Editors sagging under the weight of the gloomy tidings that clatter ceaselessly into the office on the wire, finally don't want to hear another word about mercury polluting the rivers, the shortage of oil, or Quebec's separatist movement, and the viewers or readers are penalized. Those issues simply don't get covered for a time, no matter what their urgency. It is simple cynicism that makes such subjects unsaleable, unnewsworthy. Where there is a will to cover them, there is always a fresh pair of eyes to give an old story new meaning. But the cynicism means that newsmen tend to become trendy and blasé.

Television news loses its bite, its edge. It becomes soporific, because the people putting it on the air don't really care. It becomes disconnected trivia, strings of visual non-sequiturs. We fail to put historic developments into perspective, fail to sense the drama in ordinary lives, fail to grab viewers by the shirtfront and demand that they listen. We have "cried wolf" too often. We have cheapened the language and the medium because we have run out of superlatives.

For the viewer, the TV newscast becomes a comfortable background blur of sound and picture. People tend to woolgather or chat or read the paper while the television drones on before them. But receiving the news is not intended to be, and cannot be, a totally passive activity. It will never be what the BBC thought that broadcast news was going to be, however, when, in November 1924, the first plummy-voiced announcer prefaced the first Birmingham broadcast with a kind of service message to listeners.

"It is my intention tonight," he intoned, "to read these bulletins twice, first of all rapidly and then slowly, repeating, on the second occasion, wherever necessary, details upon which listeners may wish to make notes."

It is not the viewer's fault if television news does not move him to make notes. It is television's failure to communicate, and this is due partly to its reliance on a kind of journalistic shorthand, which puts people to sleep and makes today's news a prisoner of yesterday's newscast.

Indiscriminate use of phrases like "energy crisis," "national unity," "law and order," "the business community," do evoke images in the minds of the audience and do save time. But they also tend to drape everything in a mantle of sameness and they signal the viewer that no fresh ground is about to be broken. Anyone who doubts the truth of the foregoing has only to leave the country for a month, and pick up the newspapers or turn on his favourite newscast when he returns. Thanks to the recurring phrases of current journalism, it is sometimes hard to imagine that he's been away.

But the sins of television news, like the sins of the newspapers, go much deeper. We accept far too much of what we are handed without questioning. This can be dangerous because the politicians do the same thing. Successive waves of Canadian government continue to prove that it is not in the vanguard of Canadian thought. It is somewhere between the middle and the end. It does not lead; it follows. I do not believe it is simply because politicians are afraid of leaving the voters behind. I think the problem goes deeper than that. I think it is because by and large they are out of touch, and out of ideas. Canadian journalism, television in particular, does little to help create an active intellectual society, or encourage new approaches. One of the results is that the things that are not debated in the average political campaign are often more important than the things that are. We leave the agenda almost entirely to exhausted politicians.

This tendency to accept things as they are, partly because of the broadcasters' and publishers' timidity, and partly because of our own intellectual conservatism, means that we have not really provided an adversary press, although the traditionalists, viewing analysis and opinion with alarm, seem to believe that we have already gone too far.

In *Harper's* magazine in 1978, Tom Bethell took dead aim at the big American media, and, it seems to me, managed to score a direct hit on the Canadian media with the same salvo.

"I believe," Bethell wrote, "that the most important element, in their handling of the news, is something which one at first is in danger of not noticing at all. I refer to the way in which the news organizations in question are above all relentlessly and strenuously impartial in their presentation of political events. They don't take sides. Having chosen the only important side – that of big government and all its works – the media can afford an Olympian stance with regard to the mere squabbling of factions."

In Canada, the Canadian news media "relentlessly" gives equal time to the Liberals, the Progressive Conservatives, and the New Democrats, who all support, to a remarkably similar degree, big government and all its works. Their philosophies span the political spectrum from about "L" to "M." We never raise the question of whether any of these parties should be allowed to put their hands on the tiller.

Television and newspapers accept with hardly a quibble the idea that the rising expectations of the population are reasonable and resist any politician who dares to suggest otherwise. The media manages to convey the notion that full employment is both possible and desirable in an increasingly technological world; that farmers on a starving planet should be encouraged, even forced, to produce less so that prices will remain high; that development and protection of the ecology are mutually exclusive. By and large, the media avoids new and uncomfortable ideas like radioactive fallout, and either hoots and jeers with the multitude when a political leader is courageous enough to put a new notion forward, or simply maintains a comfortable silence. By its stolid acceptance of the status quo, the Canadian media has helped to create a stifling national climate which actually discourages bold new approaches to monumental new problems. And even then, there are times when it fails to relay the status quo accurately. The stuff that gets published and broadcast as fact is often, quite literally, unbelievable.

As anyone with experience on a public platform would testify, simple accuracy is a major journalistic problem. Providing a text of one's remarks pretty well ensures the accuracy of any quotations that are used, but it doesn't ensure that the most important points will be quoted, that they'll be reported in the right context, or that the reporter will understand what it is you're trying to say.

One of the disadvantages of being a television anchorman is that I am often asked to speak, and I am reported these days with alarming frequency. It is a painful process, but a just one. Every time I am misquoted, misrepresented, or misunderstood, I wonder how many times in the course of my own journalistic career I have done the same thing to someone else.

I remember an episode in my early days as a reporter, in the mid-fifties, in Montreal. Blair Fraser, a friend of the family at whose knee I had often sat spellbound, was giving a speech to the Montreal Canadian Club, I think on a trip he had just completed to the Middle East. To my delight, I was assigned to cover it for the *Montreal Star*.

I had entered Canadian journalism in the days when some kind of shorthand or speedwriting had only just ceased to be a standard requirement, and just before the transistorized tape recorder. Fraser, who was one of the best off-the-cuff speakers I've ever heard, had no text.

And so, when he began to speak, I scrambled furiously to get it down on paper, often losing the drift of what he was saying at that moment, as I tried to record what he had said the moment before. I wound up with a wild tangle of notes – some of which was précis and some of which was direct quote. When I tried to write a story based on this muddle, I was often uncertain as to which was his version and which was mine.

The published account of Fraser's speech was a pretty slipshod affair. This was due largely to simple incompetence. I wasn't a very good reporter, and I didn't know the subject, an iron-bound formula for failure. I heard through the family grapevine from Ottawa that Blair had been disappointed in the story, and so I told the family to be sure to tell him that the desk had butchered it, a time-honoured reporter's ploy when the subject objects to what's been written.

In this case, it was perfectly true. But they butchered something, which was a mutilated carcass to begin with, and when the desk had done with it, it would have been hard to determine where my own butchery ended and theirs began. I often think of what I did to Blair Fraser when I am irritated by what someone has done to me twenty-five years later.

From the point of view of someone being quoted, anything less than the complete text of his remarks or interview is likely to be somewhat short of the ideal. If the thrust of what he said is accurately reported, that is at least satisfactory. But few people are able to take much comfort from the fact that at least the reporter spelled their names the right way.

I share in the agony of Daniel Schorr, formerly of CBS News, who himself became newsworthy after he leaked a special congressional report on the CIA to a New York newspaper, the *Village Voice*. Schorr had given the report to the *Voice* because CBS was not interested. It was not the kind of document that could easily be handled on television.

For much of 1976, Schorr lived in a state of siege, a siege mounted by the Washington Press Corps, CBS and Congress. In September, just after a successful appearance before the House Ethics Committee, which had voted not to prosecute him for leaking the report, Schorr got a call from his old CBS colleague Mike Wallace, who wanted him to appear on ''60 Minutes'' to talk about his story. Euphoric after his victory before the committee, Schorr agreed.

The taped interview lasted an hour and a quarter. Thirteen minutes of it eventually appeared on ''60 Minutes,'' and in it, Schorr was assassinated. Wallace had begun the taped interview session with an introductory statement in which he professed his ''profound admiration'' for Schorr's conduct throughout the whole sorry affair. But that and the first third of the interview, in which they discussed the responsibilities of the reporter, was cut. What was left in was the dirt, the tangled web of Schorr's relationship with his colleagues at CBS. In the edited version, Schorr lost much of his chance to give his side of the story.

''My big mistake,'' Schorr later told the *New York Times Magazine*, ''was in not insisting that the interview be done live or taped to time.'' (An interview done ''to time'' is conducted to a predetermined length and run uncut.)

''As somebody who'd been on the other side – who had, at various times, had to talk people into interviews and then maintained control of the interview, excerpting only what I wanted–I saw all the techniques of television turned around and applied against me.''

What's important about that for Canadians is that impression-able people in television here take a lot of their cues from the Americans. We are still living, for example, with a herd of middle-aged newsreaders in this country who sound like David Brinkley, a holdover from the days when the Huntley-Brinkley was the top American newscast. Even Harvey Kirck sometimes adopts the abrupt, staccato delivery and unnatural emphasis of David Brink-ley. Like a catchy tune, it's a hard cadence to get out of your head. And there is now a wave of John Chancellor aficionados upon us, using a casual lilting whine that is only a bad parody of the pro they're emulating.

And Mike Wallace, who used every move in the book on Daniel Schorr, has become something of the *beau ideal* for young Canadian interviewers. It's not the fact that Wallace is aggressive that alarms me. His interview style appeals to me neither as a newsman nor a viewer, but that's a matter of taste. What worries me about Wallace is that he has no regrets about what he did to Daniel Schorr, apparently. All's fair in love, war, and "60 Minutes."

As far as I'm concerned, there are two important ethical principles for interviews, principles I have not always followed. The first is that you know something about the man or woman you're going to interview. The second is that if you know you're going to be critical of the interviewee, you must make your feelings and your criticisms very clear while you are face to face during the interview. In other words you've got to be informed and you've got to be fair.

Wallace was informed enough in the Schorr interview, but he wasn't fair. He suckered him. He told him what a great guy he was, led him gently down the garden path, and then shoved him into a rose bush. That technique, if you can call an ambush a technique, is going to get all of us in trouble.

We cannot possibly, in television news, carry all interviews live, or film or tape them to time. We simply haven't got the space. And so we must be able to persuade the people we interview that if we pull no punches we will at least put our cards on the table.

In Canada, however, we err more often in the other direction. We tend to get too close to the people we're covering. For reporters on beats – police, the courts, city hall, the legislature, Parliament – this has always been troublesome. The traditionalists consider it vital to have "contacts" in the area they're covering – people close to the news, who will tip them off when something big is breaking, and who don't mind seeing their own names in print or their faces on the air, from time to time, as a kind of pay-off. The drawback to this kind of mutual back-scratching is that the reporter becomes dependent, on someone he is supposed to be covering, for favours.

Often, reporters become too friendly with their contacts in a social way. And, if the contact gets into trouble, or makes a mistake, there is a natural human tendency on the reporter's part to see it his way, even to participate in the cover-up which may follow. This kind of mushiness has been prevalent in Canadian journalism for too long.

For years there has been an unwritten law that journalists should not publish or broadcast the names of politicians or other public figures who have trouble with alcohol, who chase women, or who aren't bright enough for their offices. It's a strange kind of double standard in a society that permits pornography in the magazine racks of the corner store. This unwritten code may be due in part to the journalists' feeling that there but for the grace of God go we, but it's a bad business. And, fortunately, the old code is beginning to break down.

But as a profession, it is still a timid one. We are afraid of the courts, because most of us don't understand enough about the legal process; afraid of libel, because few of us are absolutely certain about what it is; afraid of angering and offending people. And this at a time when the only thing we should be afraid of is getting it wrong.

Of that, we're not sufficiently fearful. For several months, the Toronto media, Global in particular, carried stories about the anti-nuclear feeling in the town of Port Hope, a Lake Ontario community about fifty miles east of Toronto. The stories began when it was discovered that a school had been erected on a site that contained radioactive fill, waste material that had been dumped by Eldorado Nuclear Limited in the dawn of the age of nuclear power, years earlier.

Global talked to some of the community activists involved, parents, and people who lived near the school. And the impression that emerged was that Port Hope felt hard done by, suspicious, and very much opposed to the nuclear industry and all its works. Port Hope, as it turned out, was much more hard-headed than that.

When Eldorado finally decided to locate a new uranium refinery in Hope Township, Port Hope was ecstatic, and the politicians were falling all over themselves to take part of the credit for the nuclear decision. The impression left by the Global coverage was wrong.

I sometimes wonder where the news business would be if we couldn't carry denials. The trouble is if you quote someone often enough, denying that some unflattering charge is true, people come to believe there is something to it. It isn't the denial, but what was being denied that people remember. Running a denial of some charge by an agency other than one's own news service may be perfectly correct editorially. But if the original charge has not been carried on an earlier newscast, a producer ought to consider whether the story should be run at all.

Increasingly, there is an awareness in the industry that we are making too many mistakes. We tend to blame this on the increasing complexity of the society we're trying to cover, and instead of trying to hire better general reporters we try to hire specialists. This response, in my view, has been wrong. We have specialists in science, business, labour-management relations, investigation, and even, as shame-faced editors will admit, for lack of a better phrase, "life-styles." Specialists can be useful, but only if they are able to avoid the problems of the beat system, and remain journalists and communicators first.

The specialists have to be gifted, dedicated people, able to apply the journalistic embrace, in which you get close to something while keeping it at arms' length. The specialist must make himself privy to the ideas and the language of his subject, but not to the point that he begins to share the difficulty of the expert in communicating it. He must remain a layman in at least one part of his mind, a layman who can draw out the expert and force him to state his case in plain English. And still there are risks, not only that the specialist will become something of an apologist for his chosen field, but that the editor or producer in charge will tend to abrogate his own responsibilities in the specialist's area of interest. There is a temptation for an editor with a stable of specialists to stop worrying about understanding those fields they cover, and leave it up to the people who know, who at that point may not be able to see the forest for the trees. So if we appoint too many specialists at this point, I think we're getting ahead of ourselves. What we need most desperately are good general reporters, the Renaissance men of news.

Watergate has had a lasting effect not only on North American politics but on North American journalism. Carl Bernstein and

Robert Woodward of the *Washington Post*, through the coverage that began with what appeared to be a simple break-in at Democratic Headquarters, have created a whole new cadre of would-be investigative reporters. American and Canadian schools of journalism have been flooded since President Nixon's resignation. It is estimated that the American schools now graduate enough students each year to fill every job in U.S. journalism – not just every available job, you understand, but every job. The situation in Canada is not much different.

The so-called "investigative reporter" is not a new concept. There have been some great ones in North American journalism. Al Goldstein, of the *St. Louis Post-Dispatch*, was a friend of mine at the United Nations in the late fifties and early sixties. While he was a campus stringer for one of the Chicago papers, he found a pair of eye glasses which turned out to be the key piece of evidence in the Leopold and Loeb case. He won a Pulitzer prize for that story while he was just a kid, and, in my view, never quite recovered from it. It was too much, too early, and I was never sure that "investigation" was Al's longest suit. Robert Reguly, the *Toronto Star* reporter, who found Gerda Munsinger alive and well in Germany, is another great investigative reporter who I have known on and off for years.

Most of them have one thing in common. To keep them well and happy, you must have something for them to investigate. And even if you have an interesting line of investigation, it may take months of fruitless digging, which never produces a single line of type or a second of air time. It isn't the sort of endeavour that the average news editor, who is usually desperate for seasoned journalists, can watch with equanimity. Television news, where staffs are more limited and where a day's work must pretty well translate into a news item, cannot afford investigative reporters at all.

In a sense, all reporting must be investigative, and if there is the kind of venality and wrong-doing in this country that was typified by Watergate, then it is not unreasonable to suppose that good general reporters will find it. It is worth remembering that both Bernstein and Woodward were on general assignment until the Watergate story began to move and the *Post* put them on it full time. The techniques they used to unravel the edges of the Watergate cover-up were general techniques, standard equipment for a good general reporter. Woodward and Bernstein may never investigate anything of that magnitude again. If they're smart, for their own peace of mind and the sake of their own development, they will never investigate in the Watergate sense again, because anything in that line from now on will be anti-climactic, and because it tends to be dead-end journalism. After breaking the Leopold-Loeb case, driving a President out of office, or finding Gerda Munsinger, what do you do for an encore? For some reason, that kind of journalistic lightning rarely seems to hit the same reporter twice.

For two or three years following the Watergate sensation, one of the Toronto dailies approached Queen's Park as if it were a branch plant of the Committee to Re-elect the President. But all they got were a series of near scandals, strong whiffs of a pork-barrelling that won't die out completely in our political system until the old guard does. And in my view, the newspaper in question did the public a disservice by wasting time and print trying to ferret out a Watergate when it could instead have been analyzing archaic government attitudes and policies which left us ill-prepared for the seventies.

That kind of reporting, which relies more on innuendo than fact, tends to be a bad thing not only for journalism, but for the political process. It has the effect of keeping good men out of politics. It helps to create a negative and acidic climate in a country which instead needs hope.

There is no doubt in my mind that there is scandal to be uncovered in Canadian government. Government is the country's biggest industry and its disbursements have become enormous. Large amounts of money tempt people and it would be unreasonable to suppose that none of our public servants and politicians has yielded to temptation. But I believe that scandal will be best uncovered not by training up an army of journalistic private eyes, but by insisting on better journalism at the general reporting level. If there is wrong-doing in government, it will eventually be uncovered by good journalists conscientiously reporting on government, by journalists who won't take a press release or a whispered trial balloon as an answer.

Jerry Goodis, vice-chairman of MacLaren Intermart, Inc., the largest advertising group in the country, had some tough things to say about the media in a magazine article entitled "The Trivia Dealers," published in *Toronto Life* in March 1979. Most of his criticisms are well-founded, although in my view, he goes much too far.

He attacks the quality of political and economic reporting in this country with good reason. He says we build straw men (Trudeau in 1968, for example) and then tear them down. We cover campaign parades but not campaign issues. We confuse fact with opinion.

Goodis quotes extensively from an American study of the 1972 presidential campaign called "The Unseeing Eye," in which two political science professors, Thomas Patterson and Robert McClure, presented a devastating statistical analysis of how much time the major networks devoted to matters of public policy. Richard Nixon, the authors found, had fifteen policy positions, and George McGovern had eleven. During two months of coverage, the total cumulative time that CBS devoted to each of Nixon's positions in the nightly network newscast was two minutes and fifteen seconds, ABC, one minute and fifty-nine seconds, and NBC, one minute and twenty-two seconds. For each McGovern position, it was thirty seconds on ABC, one minute and nine seconds on CBS and thirty-one seconds on NBC.

No serious journalist would argue with Goodis that the figures are pathetic. But Goodis makes no mention of the quality of the reporting involved, and no mention of the time the networks were able to devote to other important subjects. And he tars Canadian television with the same brush.

I think we remain more issue-oriented in this country, and I believe that some Canadian news executives have recognized that our campaign coverage hasn't been good enough. At Global, for example, we fought back in the last campaign against the media events dreamed up by outfits like MacLaren Intermart, the "photo opportunities," by putting less of our emphasis on covering the leaders, and more of it on the issues, by dealing with the political process at the riding level.

Goodis does admit that his own industry is not without its blemishes, and that it sometimes does shoddy work. He admits that advertising men sometimes overstate the case to be made for their clients' products. But he suggests that the harm done by that kind of white lie does not compare even remotely with the kind of damage that blatantly subjective reporting does to our society.

I don't agree. I know that Goodis himself has wit and integrity, but much of television advertising is not merely boastful, it is lying, pure and simple. It's not salesmanship; it's cheating. Instant coffee does not taste and smell like real coffee and anyone who tells you that it does is not telling the truth. Most children understand that from the time they are old enough to watch the weekend cartoons. And what that understanding has done to a whole generation's perception of truth is incalculable.

What television advertising has done to debase taste is still another story. In a host of television commercials, cheerful make-believe humans, who are portrayed as both cheap and stupid, would have us believe that it is perfectly acceptable in polite society to hold gay little discussions on sanitary napkins, armpits, and how toilet paper affects the human behind. We all suspect what's next.

To suggest that mediocre, opinionated journalism is as damaging to society as pimping for finance companies at a time when personal bankruptcies are spiralling upward, or trying to convince Canadians that an acceptable life-style cannot be achieved without a case of beer, when we are living with an epidemic of alcoholism, is hardly worthy of a response. One of our major problems in television news is that endless parade of smooth-talking actors and shameless celebrities, who seem to be prepared to swear to anything for a buck. It debases the currency everywhere in television, news included.

Television news has always had problems that are unique to the medium. There can be silence on the screen, but not for long. We can continue to function without a report track, without natural sound, without music. But we can't live without pictures. As Eric

Barnouw points out in his book *Tube of Plenty*, that has been a problem from the beginning. Barnouw talks about television news in 1953, when the Camel News Caravan's John Cameron Swayze, later made famous for his Timex commercials, was the leading "Cronkiter" for millions of Americans.

"A favorite pronouncement of the day," Barnouw writes, "was that television had added a new dimension to newscasting. The truth of this concealed a more serious fact: the camera, as an arbiter of news value, had introduced a drastic curtailment of the scope of news. The notion that a picture was worth a thousand words meant, in practice, that footage of Atlantic City beauty contest winners, shot at some expense, was considered more valuable than a thousand words from Eric Sevareid on the mounting tensions in Southeast Asia. Analysis, a staple of radio news in its finest days, was being shunted aside as non-visual."

Comment is rare in Canadian network television. Oddly enough, the same broadcast executives who see nothing wrong with allowing a newsreader to do a commercial seem to believe that the expression of opinion somehow damages the credibility of the man who delivers it. From my own experience, it has the opposite effect. If people are aware of a newscaster's opinions, they have a better idea of how his biases relate to their own. They tend to add to, or subtract from what he has to say on a given subject to arrive at what they perceive as the appropriate colouration of truth, the same way that astute readers of *Time* magazine used to discount everything in it by remembering that the man who owned it was Henry Luce. If the newscaster tries to conceal his convictions, they show in subtle ways anyway. We are not automatons, and the viewers know it.

But there has been a tradition in this country, because broadcasting is perceived as a public trust, to keep opinions out of the news. In my view, it may be safe, but it is also unnatural and unhealthy.

Tom Gould, who now does a weekly hour of news analysis for Global, came under attack in the spring of 1979 for a program he'd done as the federal election campaign got under way. I thought that the attack, by interested politicians, was unfair. Although some of

Gould's remarks did reveal an anti-government bias, they were openly and honestly expressed, and based on years of critical analysis rather than allegiance to any one party.

Gould said that Trudeau had announced the election after months of "dithering," a term I suppose most Liberals found offensive, despite the fact that most of the candidates and party workers had been saying the same thing privately for months. The country had been poised for election for nearly a year by then, waiting for the moment when the polls or the seat of his pants told the Prime Minister he could win. If that wasn't dithering, what was it? Under the circumstances, dithering was not so much a comment as straight reporting.

Gould also said that in announcing the election, the Prime Minister had spoken "airily" of the issues, surely a legitimate adverb in any description of Trudeau's cool, off-hand style with the media.

"Trudeau," Gould added, "came on like an ad-man's dream — full of empty words about a decade of development and the quality of life..." A bit cynical, perhaps, but surely this too was fair comment in a country that had lived through "Sixty Days of Decision," and the "Just Society," without any discernible improvement either in the government's ability to make up its mind or in the quality of justice available to Canadians at large.

Gould himself, writing about the demise of CTV's "Backgrounder" in *TV Guide*, defended opinion on television. He wrote in part:

"The essential purpose of editorials is to provoke the viewer, listener or reader to think about an issue. The effect is not, as many suspect, to warp or twist the thoughts of those receiving the opinion."

Gould made the point that despite his own "Backgrounder," most Canadian newspaper editorials, and the majority of their MPs, Canadians continued to want capital punishment.

"There exists in this country," he wrote, "a large body of opinion that holds that Canadian people cannot be safely exposed to ideas, a belief that in some way they are incapable of drawing their own conclusions, making up their own minds, no matter what they hear or read.

"In this elitist view, there are 23 million idiots out there, with sponges in the place of brains, ready to soak up any madcap idea that comes within reach. I do not share that view. If I did, I would never have ventured in front of a microphone."

He concluded the article with a warning:

"Our television networks, Global excepted, have opted out of news commentary in fear of, or to curry favour with government. Perhaps one day they will remember that the historic struggle for freedom of the press was fought not for the right to report news but rather for the right to publish opinion."

I don't believe that everyone's opinion is valid grist for the television mill. At Global, we don't allow people to express an opinion who haven't earned the right. That means restraining junior reporters who want to savage the Prime Minister on the basis of one campaign speech when they've spent the last two years on the police beat. If they want to express an opinion on the police, that's legitimate. If they've been keeping their eyes and ears open, they do have specialized knowledge, and by any reasonable human and intellectual standards are entitled to exercise their judgement professionally, either in the form of analytical reporting or as a signed editorial comment. People with specialized knowledge may even be said to have a duty to comment.

The irony is that the people in charge of news at all three Canadian networks agree that the old ideal, stupefying objectivity with a BBC accent, is dead. Late in 1978, Knowlton Nash, then head of Information Programming at the CBC, told Bob Blackburn, who was writing for TV Ontario's monthly magazine *TVO Plus*, that "objectivity is impossible" but that fairness and balance remained realistic ideals.

Blackburn noted in the same article that even Walter Cronkite had capitulated on the matter of objectivity when he finally spoke his mind about the Vietnam war. He added that viewers have always known that "assumed or inadvertent" facial expressions by newsreaders constituted editorial comment, but that the objectivity ideal was dying hard.

There are still people in the industry who believe, or who pretend to believe, that a straight-faced recital of selected facts, without any attempt to put them in perspective, constitutes editorial truth. It is a tradition that Bill Cunningham would like to see buried:

"There's no such thing as objectivity," Cunningham told Blackburn. "There's no perfect truth. What is considered objectivity is to favour the established wisdom and that is wrong. The critical analysis factor is vital. To do anything less is an abdication of journalistic responsibility – a mindless, knee-jerk cop-out."

In my view, it is also painfully artificial. The conventional wisdom insists on pasteurizing newscasts, which are supposed to reflect the realities of the day, at a time when books, movies, magazines, and even non-news television programming foam at the mouth, unchecked, without the news constraints of fairness and balance.

One of the most savage comments on the political processes at work in the 1968 Democratic Convention in Chicago was made by NBC's "Today" show, essentially a public affairs and entertainment vehicle. As the program's closing credits rolled, the viewers could see background film of Chicago policemen, grim, helmeted, busy with their nightsticks, shoving young men and women into the paddy wagon. And as the credits and the film rolled together, the voice of Frank Sinatra was heard crooning over it:

"My kind of town, Chicago is..." Whack went a billy club. "My kind of razzmatazz..."

It was extremely effective comment, but unfair comment probably. Many Democrats and many citizens of Chicago were as distressed by what had happened as the producers of the "Today" show. Surely news is a more responsible custodian of comment. Without comment and analysis news seems to have too little substance, too little grit. Like white flour, with all the interesting parts refined out of it, the product it produces tends to be bland, tasteless, and eminently forgettable. In all other walks of public life, it goes without saying that someone who doesn't have an opinion is not just disinterested, but uninterested and probably uninformed to boot. In short, he's comatose or too lazy to care. Why should television newsmen be perceived any differently?

In Britain, whose BBC was first responsible for the neutered newsreader, the reporter's role has always been quite different. Unlike North Americans, who have traditionally been trained to present their readers or viewers with the facts they need to make a judgement, and not the judgement itself, the British and Europeans have eschewed this editorial *coitus interruptus*. They make judgements not to force the public what to think, but to convince the public that newsmen think, the theory being that no one is likely to have much respect for a mere sponge.

In Harry Boyle's swansong as chairman of the CRTC on September 15, 1977, he urged broadcasters to stand up and be counted on national unity, and to make special efforts to ensure responsible reporting on that issue. And significantly, he cautioned them against "making too great a virtue of detachment," another way of saying what Edmund Burke warned us about: "The only thing necessary for the triumph of evil is for good men to do nothing."

It would be unfair to suggest that "doing nothing" is entirely a legacy of the BBC newsreader, however. We also come by it honestly from our American parent. The Americans have been so awed by the power of broadcasting that they have been blind to some of their responsibilities. David Halberstam suggests in *The Powers That Be* that almost from the beginning there was an unconscious decision to limit the autonomy of the network news shows. This was because television touched and affected the non-reading multitude, and was believed to have mystic powers even over those who could and did read. Thus caution became the hallmark of the network newscast, and their proprietors, men like Walter Cronkite, became what Halberstam calls the "prisoners" of their own enormous influence.

Eric Sevareid and others fought the notion that the realities of the network newscasts' power should force the abdication of responsibility or that the First Amendment to the American constitution, which guaranteed a free press, should not be applied to the new medium.

"Only slowly and reluctantly," he wrote, "have many publishers and editors come to accept that the notion of divisibility, the dilutability of the First Amendment simply because of technological change in the transmission of information and ideas, is an absurd and dangerous notion."

There are differences between opinion in a newspaper and opinion on television, however, which, if they do not affect the strength of the opinion, are likely to affect how it is delivered. A newspaper editorial or even a signed piece on the editorial page has a degree of anonymity which is impossible to attain on television. It is one thing to speak out against capital punishment while sheltering behind the skirts of a newspaper editorial board. It is quite another to do it on a television newscast, when the resulting vitriol is likely to be very personal.

You reap exactly as you sow, even to the tone of voice. Unless you're dealing with a particularly hot issue, you can say almost anything you like without drawing the fire of the viewers, as long as you say it nicely. But if you speak in simple, declarative sentences and let an edge creep into your voice, the switchboard will light up before you're off the air. Those who disagree with you will use simple, declarative sentences and bald, undecorated epithets over the telephone and there'll be an edge in their voices too. Delivering oneself of opinions can be a draining experience. But it is time that the networks got over their timidity.

I didn't always agree with what the *Toronto Star*'s former critic-at-large Dennis Braithwaite used to say about television. But I understood him perfectly, when he wrote in the spring of 1979, that he didn't accept broadcasters "as a legitimate part" of what he understood the Fourth Estate to be.

"With all their technological wizardry and their speed of transmission," he wrote, "radio and TV stations still don't have the clout of the print medium, most particularly the daily newspapers. Networks and stations, with some few exceptions – notably the CBC, which has inhibitions of another sort – deal in consensus and shy away from controversy. Their editorials, when they broadcast them, are shallow or meaningless."

There are those who escape, or should escape, Braithwaite's blanket condemnation. Bruce Phillips, CTV's Ottawa bureau chief, weaves raw comment into his analysis that would be an adornment to any editorial page in the country. Global's Peter Desbarats, who comes from quite a different direction than Phillips, is often so penetrating and meaningful that they wince on Parliament Hill.

But none of this, of course, frees CTV and Global from the obligation to broadcast pictures. The best comments in newscast are often based on an arresting visual story carried earlier. They seem to have more impact when they are tied directly to a visual set of facts which are still reasonably vivid in the minds of the viewers.

The pictures do have to be interesting, a fact that puts undue emphasis on the abnormal. Normal is dull, and unlike a newspaper, which is not intended to be read cover to cover, television cannot afford dull patches. Too many of those drive the viewer to change channels or shut the set off completely.

One of the problems with the whiff-bam quality of television news, is that, like the producers of half-hours and hours, the television reporter, cameraman, and film editor have some responsibility for holding the audience, handing it back to the anchorman, and, eventually, to the next reporter in the line-up. The reporter must remember that his story is only as good as his pictures. Dull, or badly cut film, and a script that is so good it could be sung, still add up to a tedious story. It is a lesson that former newspaper reporters, who continue to be the mainstay of television journalism, find it hard to learn. They must be made to understand that they have one chance at the viewer, one chance to inform him. If his attention wanders, the viewer can't go back the way a newspaper reader can if a story loses his interest or doesn't seem to make sense. It means that a television story must be unfolded logically and with unmistakable clarity. The story must be simple, but it doesn't mean that the language or the thoughts conveyed must also be elementary. Too often that results in the "see Joe run" school of reporting, which makes the viewer feel that the reporter takes him for a simpleton.

Time, and the distortion that arises from compression, is the problem that seems to get the most attention. Walter Cronkite got coverage in the newspapers, if little sympathy from CBS, in a speech he gave to a conference of the Radio and Television News

Directors' Association (RTNDA) at Miami Beach in December 1976. He likened the half-hour newscast to a "one-pound sack" and he issued a plea:

"Give us at least a two-pound sack for one hundred pounds of news every night," he said. "Now that will not be enough. There is no way we can ask the public to sit still in front of the box long enough to get all the news it needs. We will always be a complementary medium to front for those who would be fully informed.

"But with another half hour, by doubling our time, we would take a long stride towards eliminating distortion through over-compression. We would not have many more items, would not present features and extraneous interviews, but we would take a little more time with each item – enough extra time for the explanatory phrase, the 'why' and the 'how', as well as the 'who', 'what', and 'where'."

Global has an hour in its early newscast, although it is not used in precisely the way Cronkite suggests, and probably wouldn't be, even if we had the machine and the running money to fill an hour solidly with hard news. I'm not at all sure that the public would sit still for the kind of hour that Cronkite is suggesting, even with Walter Cronkite at the anchor desk.

But there is no doubt that the length of two major newscasts in this country is hopelessly inadequate. The CTV newscast is on the air for twenty minutes, but that period includes four minutes of commercials. It means that Lloyd and Harvey have about sixteen minutes between them, eight minutes apiece, a considerably lighter load than they were intended to bear. Tom Gould, then the vice-president, said, when he hired Lloyd away from the CBC, in 1976, that he hoped the network's directors would vote soon to extend the newscast from twenty to thirty minutes. Gould has long since given up the job and the fight, and any hope for a nightly half-hour now seems to be dead.

The CBC is much better, but still inadequate in my view. For its "O and O's" (The CBC's "owned" and "operated" stations), the newscast is on the air for a full twenty-five minutes. And thus, if you live in Toronto or one of the other major CBC centres, you get twenty-five minutes of news for a twenty-five-minute investment of your time, a much better deal than the one offered by CTV.

But the CBC is under the same kind of pressure from its affiliates that CTV is under from the individual station owners who also sit on the network's board of directors. At 11:30 P.M., the bulk of Canadian viewers go to bed, taking the stations' hope of commercial revenue with them. And at both networks this has engendered an indecent scramble for the handful of minutes remaining after the news and before the great disappearing act at 11:30, the "bottom of the clock."

At least until the middle of 1979, the CBC capitulated to its revenue hungry affiliates in an interesting and visible way. At the twenty-minute mark in "The National," the CBC provided a "getaway" shot of Nash – an unexplained, silent, wide-angle shot of the reader at his desk – which, for thousands of viewers dependent on a CBC affiliate, represented the end of the news. The shot was up only for a couple of seconds, and then for the O and O audience, the newscast continued. They've dropped that shot now, but I think they have provided the affiliates with a more sophisticated way to get out and earn some more money before the commercial witching hour ends at 11:30. It means that in effect, the CBC line-up editor has to work within a twenty-minute time frame. The most important stories of the day have to be structured into that first twenty-minute package, or the affiliates' viewers are ill-served. This sometimes means that despite the best efforts of the CBC's line-up editors, the last five minutes are blown on light features and other trivia. The twenty-minute newscast and the five-minute trailer are still better than CTV's sixteen minutes, but the taxpayers deserve better from their national network.

In the view of many sane Canadians, the timing of the national newscasts is a more serious flaw than their abbreviated length. For many people, particularly those living in the suburbs, who must be up early to commute, and for those who live in the towns and country, who follow a schedule closer to nature, 11:00 P.M. is too late for a national newscast.

When he quit "The National" to open the Nairobi bureau, in the fall of 1978, Peter Kent delivered himself of two years of smouldering resentment about the 11:00 P.M. time slot of "The National." He called it an "ungodly" hour, and pointed out that 85 per cent of the country's television sets were turned off by then.

Of course the national newscasts are at 11:00 *because* 85 per cent of the nation's sets are dark by then, not despite it. On all three networks at the moment, the heavy-viewing hours are reserved primarily for money making, and trash has always sold better than news, although in Canada, that proposition has never been adequately tested. The largest audience is available between 7:00 and 11:00 P.M., the golden zone, which is why newscasts are scheduled at either end. The networks are loath to sacrifice any of that time to what might be considered a public service as long as there is a buck to be made. The public's newly entrenched belief that it has a right to entertainment has not been lost on TV's salesmen.

In the four and a half years that Global ran its late news at 10:00 P.M., it built an intensely loyal and highly vocal following. Unfortunately, the numbers never matched the quality of the audience. Just before we moved the newscast to 11:00 P.M., we had about a 6-per-cent share of the Ontario market, which meant that in commercial terms, we were starving to death.

The percentage was low despite the fact that in the course of a week, at one period, Global news attracted almost a million different Ontario viewers. What this meant to people who analyzed the ratings was that although a lot of people said they watched the 10:00 P.M. news, in actual fact they watched it perhaps two times a week. On other evenings, social commitments, sporting events, recreation, or blockbuster entertainment on other channels intervened.

After four and a half years, despite my own strenuous objections, the network decided it had had enough, and moved the late newscast into competition with the giants, at 11:00 P.M. The uproar was and continues to be enormous. Pierre Camu, the chairman of the CRTC, wrote an angry personal letter to Paul Morton, the president of Global, shortly after word of the move leaked out in the late summer of 1978. In it, he accused Global of breaking a trust and depriving viewers of a program alternative. But the CRTC, which has limited power to tell a broadcaster what to broadcast, has little control over when. Primarily, it can only set minimums for Canadian content, pass judgement on matters of taste, and hold the broadcasters to their individual promises of performance. Later, in the spring of 1979, when Global applied to the CRTC for licence renewal, one of the commissioners, Roy Faibish, warned Global that by making the move to 11:00 it had placed its licence in jeopardy. On August 9, the licence was renewed anyway.

Understandably, the viewers we had seduced into an early newscast were angry too. The network and I received hundreds of letters and telephone calls from people who furiously described themselves as "former" viewers. But what happened to the numbers, at least initially, followed the schedulers' predictions. When we first made the move, the ratings fell off to about half of what they had been for the 10:00 P.M. slot, 3 per cent of the audience as opposed to 6 per cent. Within three months, however, the ratings were back up to about 5 per cent, admittedly of a much smaller audience, but a big enough share to justify the move. In time, it appeared that Global would recover the share it had at 10:00 and it had opened up the 10:00 to 11:00 P.M. time slot for a program like "Baretta." You can fault their taste, but not their arithmetic.

It is that same arithmetic that ensures that CTV will remain at 11:00 P.M. (it too tried 10:00 P.M. when it first went on the air) and that the CBC will remain there just as long as it is dependent on commercial revenue to make up the shortfall between the government appropriation and its operating budget. There was talk for a time of carrying the 10:00 P.M. feed of "The National" to the Maritimes live in Vancouver (7:00 P.M. West Coast time) to gauge audience response. And there was renewed talk in the summer of 1979 about carrying "The National" at 9:00 P.M. But it will remain talk as long as the CBC wants a big audience for its major newscast, and as long as it needs the money it now makes on prime-time American junk.

In Canada, the CBC's affiliates and CTV's individual stations have come to regard the early time period – 6:00 P.M. to 7:00 P.M. – as a time for local and regional newscasts, and they are not anxious to let go of that. But the Americans realized at the beginning that it had to be the other way – national news early, local news at 11:00. It may be that we will come to that eventually in Canada, twenty-five years after we first discovered that most people were bored by our indecision and had gone to bed.

CHAPTER TEN

Freedom
and the Law

There is an all-pervasive gutlessness about Canadian journalism that becomes most apparent when our reporters leave the country. We tend to be absolutely fearless about reporting unsavoury truths from Rhodesia or Zimbabwe, or even from Chicago. Much of the time we do not maintain the same high standard of truth at home. Tony Lukas of the *New York Times* had a name for the journalistic bluntness and tartness that is born of distance from the home base. He called it the "Afghanistan principle." George Davidson of the CBC was preaching the same principle during the FLQ crisis in 1970, when he told Canadian Press it was one thing to report such incidents in far-off countries, but "quite another" when they were in our own backyard. A professional newsman would not have admitted the principle, and certainly would not have endorsed it.

I remember when the Canadian news corps in Washington rushed off to Birmingham, Alabama in 1964, to report on the doings of Eugene "Bull" Connor, the local Commissioner of Fire and Police. Connor's idea of law and order was to turn high-pressure hoses and police dogs loose on non-violent black demonstrators. I was working for the *Montreal Star* at the time, and I soon discovered that about two weeks of this was my limit. I couldn't take much larger doses of an unadulterated diet of hate and prejudice without becoming permanently sick to my stomach.

Once, after a swing to Tuscaloosa, Alabama, and Jackson, Mississippi, when I had returned to home base in Washington, I found a message waiting for me to come up to Montreal for a few days. Perhaps my distress had been showing. My editors suggested that I should plan on coming back to Canada a couple of times a year, to clear my head a little, and by doing some reporting in Canada, to renew my feel for the Canadian readership.

It struck me as a good idea, and I readily agreed. I suggested that as a first project I should do a series on discrimination and prejudice in Canada. One of the things that had continued to bother me about honest Canadian reporting on the American South was its basic hypocrisy.

In discussing the series, I mentioned the condition of our own native peoples, pointed out that French Canadians were notable by their absence in senior civil service jobs, and cited the fact that many of the country's most prestigious private clubs discriminated against Jews and other minority groups. I mentioned the Rideau Club in Ottawa, which at that time had no Jewish members, and the St. James Club in Montreal. (It wasn't until August of 1979, incidentally, that the Rideau Club accepted its first woman member.) My project outline was uneasily received, and quietly shelved. I heard no more either about the suggested series or the notion that I should come back to Canada periodically for a refresher course in Canadianism. It was the beginning of the end for me and the *Montreal Star*.

In a sense, Canadian journalism has now begun to reap a just reward for the blind eye it long turned on other people's civil liberties. By ignoring other people's rights, we have encouraged those who would curtail rights in the interest of order and efficiency to go after press freedoms.

At the time of writing, it is too early to say what kind of effect the new Clark government's proposed Freedom of Information legislation will have on the news industry's dealings with government, but I think it is fair to say that unless the media itself demonstrates more concern, the gradual erosion of rights will continue.

At Global in 1978, we had three different levels of police in our newsroom, trying to seize news film, some of which had been broadcast, and some of which consisted of "out-takes," that is film that wound up on the cutting-room floor. Our strategy for dealing with demands of this kind was fairly basic. We agreed to release film that had been on the air, because it was "published" material and hence in the public domain. We would not release the outs, on the grounds that they deserved the same kind of confidentiality as a reporter's notes. Or at least we would not release them without a warrant, a search, and non-co-operation.

On May 30, Global had a call from the Metropolitan Toronto Police, who wanted to screen film we had shot the previous day during a violent demonstration by the Union of Injured Workers outside the Queen's Park office of a provincial minister. The police revealed that they wanted to screen the film to see if they could identify a man who was alleged to have snatched and brandished an officer's pistol at some point during the brawl. We refused.

We were quite willing to tell the police that there was no film of anyone grabbing and waving a constable's sidearm. If there had been, it would have been aired, because it would have been news. But that was really beside the point.

A reporter's function is journalism, not informing. A short time previously, one of our field producers had to use a little judicious force to protect a cameraman against violent strikers. The strikers had charged that we were not only shooting film for Global but for the police. How can we refute that charge, when it is levied, if we meekly turn over our unused film to any policeman who decides to stage a fishing expedition in our newsroom? And yet, in 1978, police hit newsroom after newsroom for film, radio tapes, other broadcast material, and still photographs, and met no common front, only sporadic, unco-ordinated resistance. This despite the fact that there is no legislation in Canada that compels newsmen to give police information they have gathered in the course of their reporting. The weight of a court order is needed, and a court order, of course, can be appealed.

The same battle has been gaining momentum in the United States, where on May 31, 1978, the United States Supreme Court ruled by five to three that news-gathering agencies do not enjoy any special right to advance warning of a court-approved search by law enforcement officers, or an opportunity to contest such a search in the courts before it occurs.

The decision prompted one newspaper group in Lee, Montana, to purge its files of confidential material. The *Los Angeles Times,* appalled by the decision, noted that "we have been living in a different kind of country since May 31." On the ABC Evening News, Howard K. Smith said it best:

"When I was a young reporter at the United Press in Nazi Berlin," he recalled in his evening comment, "there was a knock at the door, and fifteen Gestapo men barged past me, began opening every desk and studying every piece of paper they could find. Six hours later they left. I remember thanking God that this couldn't happen in America. Well now it can. It is the most dangerous ruling the court has made in memory."

The decision was seen by the news media as Nixon's revenge, since during his years in office he had consistently appointed right-wing conservatives to the court, when there were vacancies in the liberal ranks chosen by previous Democratic administrations. Representative Howard Drinan, a Massachusetts Democrat, proposed legislation intended to reserve the ruling, an objective in which President Carter himself concurred.

In Canada, the response has been much less determined. On the very day that the American uproar was beginning, Waterloo Regional Police Chief Syd Brown arbitrarily imposed a news blackout on the *Kitchener-Waterloo Record. Record* reporters were denied their usual access to police headquarters until the ban was lifted. The blackout was imposed because the newspaper had published two photographs from police files which had been slipped to the paper by a disgruntled department contact. The blackout was lifted after two days, but the principle was allowed to stand, at least in legal terms. The newspaper took no subsequent court action to secure a ruling against the infringement. And neither did anyone else.

If the arbitrary implementation of such restrictions by the police and by the courts continues to go unchallenged by Canadian media, the new Freedom of Information Bill will have little real effect. If, on the other hand, the news media rouses itself from its torpor and decides to fight, everyone is likely to benefit.

The kind of natural conflict that arises when a free press struggles to stay free, and police forces seek freedom to pursue the truth, is the kind of conflict that keeps both institutions honest. It forces the press to examine its rights in relation to the greater good of society as a whole, and it forces the police to review their methods in relation not only to the rights of the media but to the rights of ordinary citizens. The news media must have second thoughts in its pursuit of the story, and the police must have second thoughts in their pursuit of the people they're trying to bring to book. There are no second thoughts in a totalitarian society.

Quite obviously, Canadian police departments need watching, as the Macdonald inquiry into RCMP wrong-doing and Ontario's Krever Commission into the confidentiality of health records made clear. There seems to be an increasingly widespread police assumption that the ends justify the means, and worse.

In an astonishing brief submitted to the Krever Commission in June 1979, the Metropolitan Toronto Police Force admitted freely that police and medical workers frequently violated the confidentiality of health records.

"Information exchange," the brief said, "especially between hospital staff and police in routine matters. . .is invariably a casual, informal, co-operative exercise, unencumbered by the imposition and interference of formal rules.

"Whether such information exchange occurs in spite of, because of, or in ignorance of the current law, is, in a sense, an irrelevant concern. The fact that it does occur, in itself, indicates the need for it to occur."

During the previous September, the eighty senior officers attending the annual meeting of the Canadian Association of Police Chiefs in Ottawa, warned the government that proposed Freedom of Information legislation threatened police effectiveness in fighting organized crime and terrorism. They urged the government to increase, not decrease, protection of confidential police information.

Their concern was understandable, but the chiefs should have been reminded that there will always be conflict between their own natural desire for efficiency and the aims of a free society. The most effective police forces operate in closed societies. And for us, what is reasonable efficiency and reasonable freedom can only be determined by trial, error, and open debate.

Such a pragmatic approach isn't possible unless the news media is prepared to fight the erosion of freedom of the press and human rights generally. There can be no dialogue, no meaningful trial and error, without a free press struggling to preserve that freedom. A free press doesn't mean an irresponsible one, however. The press must conform to the ethics of responsible journalism, and it must also conform to the law of the land. But it cannot be supine in the face of a bad law. It must challenge bad laws the way that thoughtful men used to challenge bad kings. Kings were the law before the evolution of constitutional monarchy, and where would parliamentary democracy be today if they had not been challenged?

The Official Secrets Act, as it was applied against Peter Treu and the *Toronto Sun,* is a law that should not have been allowed to stand. For the Trudeau government to charge the *Sun* and not the other news agencies who also published excerpts from the ''Top Secret'' document, was to leave itself open to the charge that it was acting vindictively against a newspaper whose editorial policy opposed it.

The Canadian act was derived in part from the seventy-year-old British Secrets Act, under which journalists could in theory be prosecuted for reporting the number of cups of tea consumed per week by one of Her Majesty's ministries.

In 1971, London's *Sunday Telegraph* was prosecuted under a section of the British act, which is almost identical to Section Four of the Canadian act. The Labour government had insisted throughout the civil war between Nigeria and breakaway Biafra that arms shipments to the Nigerian government were no larger than the amounts being shipped before the trouble broke out. The *Telegraph* published a confidential official report which gave the lie to the government's claims. It indicated that arms shipments had been increased substantially. The government hit the roof and took the *Telegraph* to court.

In his summing up, the judge hearing the case, Mr. Justice Caulfield, had this to say:

"You must work on the basis, members of the jury, that there is no censorship in this country. There is no duty in law – I want to make this absolutely plain – there is no duty in law for any editor or any newspaper to go running to Whitehall to print an article or to print news." The jury retired for lunch and returned with a verdict of not guilty.

In the case against the *Toronto Sun*, the judge who presided over the preliminary hearing, Mr. Justice Waisberg, made much the same kind of point. He said that although Canadian security was of paramount importance, the press must not be muzzled by the act, because its "warning bark" was necessary to maintain a free society.

He pointed out that the act, passed as the country was being plunged into war in 1939, needed to be redrafted completely. And he ruled that the document which got the *Sun* into hot water – an RCMP paper optimistically headed "Top Secret – For Canadian Eyes Only" – was "shopworn and no longer secret" by the time of publication. He threw out the charges against the *Sun*.

After the decision, *Sun* editor Peter Worthington described it as a "vindication of common sense." He said he realized there was a need for an Official Secrets Act of some sort, but that the present law was an abomination.

"It's a criminal statute," he told reporters, "designed to get traitors and spies. I feel like neither a traitor nor a spy." He added that the act should not be used to "get journalists" or "go after a newspaper a particular politician may not like."

The irony is that it was Mr. Justice Waisberg who perceived that the media's "warning bark" was in danger. The media itself appeared to be complacent, although it might have seen things differently if the *Sun*'s executives had been ordered to stand trial, and if there had been a conviction.

Ironically, as Tory MP Gerald Baldwin (PC Peace River) laboured on behalf of Peter Treu and the party's position paper that

196

gave rise to the proposed Freedom of Information Bill, the news media tended to bury him in the back pages. We have accepted the government's protective attitude towards information, part of our parliamentary legacy, for far too long.

Twenty years ago, a brash young External Affairs information officer at Canada's United Nations Mission in New York, put it succinctly in a casual conversation one day at a UN bar.

"You know," he mused over a scotch, "our jobs are diametrically opposed. Yours is to gather information and mine is to suppress it."

Daniel Schorr, while appearing before a congressional committee in his own defence, put the journalistic argument:

"The press, as I see it in the Constitution, was given the function of monitoring what the government does, of giving people information, even information which may not at that moment be popular...There is a necessary tension between what you do and what I do...Once a secret is out, if you go and try to chase it down, and call it back, and punish the one who had published it, then I think you have gone too far...How in God's name can we expose the secrets of government and let the people know what the government is doing if we can only expose what you say we can expose?"

The Canadian War Measures Act, which is still on the books, has been suspect even longer than the Official Secrets Act. It was used to intern innocent Japanese-Canadians during the Second World War, an infamous piece of discriminatory injustice, and it was used again by Prime Minister Trudeau to put down a state of "apprehended insurrection," the much-vaunted double kidnapping of 1970.

It isn't just bad laws that journalists should be fighting, but bad rulings by the courts. Increasingly in the coverage of court cases, newsmen have been barred from some stage of the proceedings. The new judicial rule of thumb appears to be: "When in doubt, throw them out." At Global, we have resisted the trend at every opportunity. Twice recently, we have appeared with counsel to appeal such rulings. But by and large we have stood alone.

Global defied the federal government's gag regulation, which prohibited public discussion of Ottawa's extremely suspect role in the 1972-75 uranium cartel. The regulation, which set a maximum penalty of a $10,000 fine and two years in jail, was not invoked.

But when Conservative MPs applied to have the courts throw out the gag regulation, Ontario Chief Justice Gregory Evans ruled against them. The effect of his ruling was that MPs were free to debate a subject like the uranium cartel in the House, in accordance with parliamentary privilege. But the press and broadcast media were not free to report the proceedings, and Canadians in general were not free to discuss them, without the risk of prosecution.

The chief justice was, of course, dealing with the narrow area of parliamentary privilege, and there is no reason to question the judgement. He strongly reaffirmed Parliament's traditional freedom of debate, within the rules of the House, and he made it clear that the government had no right to prevent MPs from making disclosures in the Commons. But their parliamentary privilege did not extend to the reporters or anyone else discussing speeches outside the Commons. Nor did it allow an MP to relay facts to his constituents.

"If this is the case," the *Toronto Star* noted in an editorial, "it is intolerable in principle and idiotic in practice. It would mean, for example, that a television network carrying a debate live would be liable to prosecution if an MP blurted out some piece of information that the government was trying to suppress by legislation."

It does not appear to have been an issue that worried the networks, however. The *Star*'s denunciation was somewhat lonely.

The media tends to be in awe of the courts. We stand back and leave the lawyers alone. Our failure to intervene has meant that the law has been largely free of the pressures of a changing society, and it has become an increasingly archaic institution. This is not a view that the profession itself welcomes.

"Surely you have reached a stage," I told a group of lawyers recently, "when the traditional trappings of the legal profession, originally intended to dignify the law, have instead made it the object of deep public suspicion and a certain amount of fearful ridicule. Surely it is your duty as lawyers to come out from behind that frustrating barricade of legalese, and deliver your opinions in plain English. If you continue to hide behind that barricade, you will further fuel the suspicion that you are maintaining it simply to confuse the general public and ensure that you will continue to make a living.''

I went on to make the point that cameras had been allowed into the House of Commons, and surely it was time for them to be allowed into courtrooms. It has always escaped me why the principle of a camera is any different than that of a reporter's notebook or an artist's sketch pad. It's true that in this stage of our development, the camera still tends to create news, and might be expected to encourage some additional histrionics on the part of counsel and witnesses. But the cameras in Parliament have not had that effect, and surely good judges can be expected to maintain order and proper decorum in their own courts. If cameras were operated under a strict set of rules, I see no reason why they should turn the proceedings into the kind of circus that so many jurists seem to fear.

''You've all seen the pathetic way we have to cover court cases,'' I reminded the lawyers. ''The reporter does a stand-up piece to camera outside the building. We voiceover film of the key figures, as they emerge from the front door, and depending on whether they are part of the prosecutor's team or the defence's team, walk boldly towards the cameras, smiling, or flee to the left or right over the lawns screened by the tail of their raincoats.''

I pointed out that we had to resort to artists' sketches, which were of more value to the accused than anyone else, in that his own mother, let alone the neighbours, usually wouldn't recognize him. But I was heard out in stony silence.

I have to admit that the fact that cameras are still barred from the courtrooms, a practice that helps to sustain the public's lack of confidence in our system of justice, and its relevance, is not so much the lawyers' fault as ours. Understandably, perhaps, the idea horrifies many of those who have been called to the bar. We haven't pushed hard enough, or mustered our arguments, and we have not managed to make a good case for the presence of cameras as prospective agents for legal public relations.

Freedom of the press is not something for which we can look to the world at large for sustenance. For the most part, it is an English-speaking tradition that has been adopted only in comparatively recent times by the rest of the western world, and not at all by many of the new nations.

Arthur Bryant, the great English social historian, in *Years of Victory, 1802 - 1812*, writes of Napoleon Bonaparte's attitude towards the press. After the revolution, he imposed a censorship even more rigorous than that of the Bourbons. The French didn't seem to care greatly.

"It was difficult for Bonaparte to conceive of a newspaper not being subject to police supervision," Bryant wrote. "Yet in England, opposition and refugee journals published the most outrageous things about him without the government stirring a finger. He used to lie in his bath every morning and have them read by an interpreter; at any particularly outrageous passage he would bang the side of the bath with the guide rope and shout furiously: *'Il en a menti.'*"

Napoleon was not the last reader to discover that on occasion Fleet Street lied. Nor was he the only European to be astounded at the extent of its freedom. Another was Prince Alexander, son of the Grand Duke Louis the Second of Hesse, and the man who eventually founded the Mountbatten line. The prince, having worn out his welcome at the Russian Imperial Court, paid his first visit to London in 1850.

According to Douglas Liversidge, in his book *Prince Philip, First Gentleman of the Realm*, Prince Alexander was astonished by the liberal ways of the English. After visiting the editorial offices of *The Times*, he wrote to his sister in St. Petersburg.

"It is utterly amazing," he noted, "how the journalists can write freely about the Royal Family, even about the private lives of Queen Victoria and her consort in a newspaper which is being read by everybody."

The United Nations Educational, Scientific, and Cultural Organization (UNESCO), which has 146 member nations, has recently been wrestling with a draft declaration on the mass media, which fills western hearts with horror. The original draft, which had Soviet approval, implied government control, and worse. It assigned to journalists political and diplomatic responsibilities.

Although as far as I know, no Canadian journalists were directly involved, the federal government needed no prompting. John Roberts, then the Secretary of State, flatly rejected the draft. He said that Canadians did not believe that politicians or public servants should have anything to say in the management, direction, or correction of the media.

The International Press Institute, a western-dominated world press association, at a general assembly in Athens in June 1979, also rejected a UNESCO draft for the "protection" of journalists. Under the UNESCO proposal, full-time reporters would have been given special identification to protect them from interference by their own governments and others. But the identification would have been issued only if a reporter agreed to a code of conduct which spelled out journalistic morality and prescribed social awareness. The institute saw it all as a thinly-veiled mechanism for controlling the world's press.

So it's no good looking elsewhere for help. It's a fight that we'll have to wage on our own.

CHAPTER ELEVEN

The Future

Television is teetering on the edge of another revolution. As in any revolution, it is still uncertain at this stage what will emerge at the far end. But in the United States, there is a growing suspicion that the days of the four networks – NBC, CBS, ABC, and PBS – may be numbered. Satellites and home-recording devices (VCRs and the new discs), cable systems and fibre optics have begun to shake the industry to its foundations. The concepts of prime time and mass programming may be on their way out. American superstations, like Ted Turner's WTCG in Atlanta, are distributing programs by satellite to cable systems all over the country. Even now, Turner's programming reaches more than five million households in forty-six American states. A recent article in the *New York Times Magazine* predicts that by 1990, there could be ten or even twenty satellite networks operating in the United States, serving as many different interests and tastes.

This gargantuan upheaval south of us, and the probability of its having far-reaching effects on Canada, have not gone unnoticed. On October 16, 1979, the Federal Communications minister, David MacDonald, announced his intention to ask the CRTC to hold public hearings as soon as possible on satellite distribution of TV programming, and Pay TV. That's all right, as far as it goes, but I hope that the politicians keep a weather-eye on the proceedings and reserve to Parliament the right to make any decisions. There is too much at stake to rely completely on the CRTC and its limited vision. Its myopia has given us trouble before.

We are being forced to deal with the implications of the satellite revolution in a hurried way because those in authority are fearful that Canadians will be subjected to a new and uncontrolled flood of American programming. Already, with relatively simple earth stations – now being mass-produced for the backyards of North America – Canadians have begun to pick off U.S. Pay TV satellite signals. Until there is some kind of strategy and regulation, Canadian cable operators will, if they dare, be able to pirate as many as thirty-two U.S. satellite signals, which will offer first-run movies, all-news channels, sports, religious, and children's programming.

The CRTC and the politicians are not simply worried about the cultural impact of this new American programming, which they hope to temper through their control of the cable distribution systems, now being surrendered to the provinces, but about the temptation to "pirate." If piracy becomes widespread, and the backyard satellite dish at least makes that possible, it could become a potentially nasty source of friction between Canada and the United States. The only way to deal with this threat is to get into "sync" with the Americans, and inaugurate our own parallel systems. And so we in Canada are also on the brink of a revolution, the same kind of revolution that threatens the American networks.

The least that can happen, when the first satellite network comes on stream in Canada – whether it's Pay TV or otherwise – is that there will be further fragmentation in an already dangerously fragmented market. Cable was the first blow to the Canadian networks, and the licensing of Global was the second. It is distinctly possible that satellite TV could be the final blow for CTV and its fledgling competitor. For individual Canadian stations, the future is somewhat more secure. If they are clever enough to make themselves indispensable because of community-oriented information, entertainment and group-produced programming, they will probably survive. A national service, whether it continues to be beamed by microwave, or is shoved through the ether by satellite-to-ground cable systems, will not be able to displace them.

Depending on what the CRTC discovers, and the politicians decide, the Canadian networks may find it difficult to continue when the new technology overtakes them. The U.S. networks may eventually be reduced to the role of production houses, program suppliers for individual stations, satellite stations, and cable systems. Their function as broadcasters may be drawing to a close.

It won't be long before the average American viewer will be able to rely on his television set to record and store newscasts, entertainment programs, football games and movies automatically, for playback at leisure. The video cassette recorder (VCR), now being sold in limited quantities to the affluent, already offers this service in a less sophisticated way. When the new technology is in place in average American homes, the prime-time concept will be dead. Producers will no longer be competing for the viewer's time, but for his interest, and his mind. The viewer will for the first time be able to be as selective as the reader. He will be able to pick the documentary or the drama of his choice, watch the news when it is convenient, roll "fast-forward" through something that bores him, or stop it for a moment when there is someone at the door. It will give him the same freedom of choice, as applied both to time and content, that now exists for the reader of books, magazines, and newspapers.

The viewer's freedom will also change the producer's role. He will no longer be in the position of having to hold onto the audience passed to him by the producer of the previous half-hour, often on an unrelated subject at an unrelated intellectual level.

He will no longer have to pitch his product below the nation's belt, to that minority group, which programers refer to as "the wad," and which now contributes the big numbers to the rating services. "The wad" is that undiscriminating, entertainment-famished band that watches as much as ten hours of television a day.

The producer will be free to pick his audience, like a book or magazine publisher, or to mix the serious with the frivolous, like the publisher of a newspaper, secure in the knowledge that his audience will pick out only what appeals to them, like raisins from a cake.

In the final analysis, it should also make advertising less painful to the viewer. Program sophistication and commercial sophistication will have to be better matched. The audience numbers will not matter so much to the advertiser as its interests.

What excites me most about this is that it means a quality newscast, which concentrates on attracting a thoughtful, influential, and hence almost certainly affluent audience, should for the first time become a commercial possibility.

What terrifies me is that the CRTC, by moving too quickly, and using the instant pragmatism which has distinguished the rationale for Canadian broadcasting in the past, may lock us into a distribution system which hamstrings our potential. So far, attempts to establish a Canadian satellite network have been caught up in a skirmish between the broadcasters and the cable operators over who is going to get the biggest piece of the pie. And so, in the fall of 1979, Pay TV was being dangled in front of the industry in an attempt to get it to resolve its differences and hold the American wolf at bay.

It would be too bad if once again we let the medium dictate the message. The CRTC seems to be saying that the hardware is in place and we've got to figure out a way to start using it before someone else spoils everything. But if once again we let the hardware dictate what we use it for, and how we use it, it will be the CBC all over again, an unmanageable, unworkable hybrid that tries to be everything to everyone and finally satisfies no one completely. If we allow that to happen, it would be as if a plastics manufacturer arbitrarily produced a number of three-quart jugs, and the dairy industry regulated itself to fill them, without regard to whether the consuming public wanted more or less milk, or in fact might want cheese or ice cream instead.

Surely now is the time to take a hard look at the television we're getting, what it is doing to us as a society in both cultural and political terms, and then try to decide what it is we want instead. Then, and only then, it seems to me, can we talk about systems. If we ever needed a Royal Commission on Broadcasting, we need one now.

About the only factor in the situation late in 1979 that gave me any confidence at all was the character of the communications minister, David MacDonald. He was determined that this time the people of

Canada would be given a chance to say in advance what they wanted, and that what could be a golden opportunity for good television would not be sacrificed on the altar of commerical expediency. He or his successor will have to be strong, because the pressures are going to be enormous.

There is a great deal that needs correcting. I need no survey to tell me that something is wrong when serious viewers in a market like Toronto, betrayed too often by the CBC, have to watch the Public Broadcasting System's Buffalo station, or the Ontario Educational Network for much of their serious programming.

I need no survey to tell me that it's time we took a hard look at that public-private hybrid, the CBC, and the wisdom of its trying to be all things to all people, whether it continues as a microwave network, becomes a satellite network, or becomes simply a national production house.

Too much of the CBC's programming has been dictated by the fact that, for many Canadians, it has been the only television source. And in areas which are also served by the other national network, CTV, it has been seduced into a shameless race for ratings – partly because it has to compete in the marketplace for advertising revenue, which now accounts for about $70 million of its $500 million annual budget, and partly because a substantial erosion of its audience would almost certainly mean questions in the House and the risk of cutbacks in its government appropriation. The CBC has never been completely free of the degrading pressures of commercial television.

The CBC prefers to speak of its pursuit of "balanced" programming in explaining what it puts on the air, but balanced in this instance is merely a euphemism for enough of the cheap and dirty to satisfy the TV junkies, who make up the bulk of the national audience.

The corporation has responded to the increasing pressure for serious, commercial-free programming by suggesting a second network, a Canadian TV 2, to service those who feel they have a right to something more than they're getting. But that suggestion makes sense neither in economic nor program terms. Why stick the taxpayers with the cost of another network, while the CBC continues its $430-million, publicly-financed assault on the private broadcasters with the other? And why, if you were going to set up another network, would you entrust its operation to a group of people who have proved rather conclusively that they can't manage the one they've got?

Under the existing arrangement, there would be a ferocious backlash if the CBC were forced to drop commercials and popular programming and concentrate on excellence. But the people who prefer junk programming, "the wad," are in the minority. Their influence is disproportionate because they watch so many hours of television. Increasingly, by looking for ratings, the CBC caters less and less to the more discriminating majority.

If the CBC were able to abandon its commercial rationale, the benefits would be enormous, not just to the bulk of the nation's citizens but to the industry. If the two commercial networks had access to the $70 million plus in advertising revenues, which are now used to prop up the CBC, it would soften the effects of fragmentation brought about by cable. And it would then be reasonable for the CRTC to insist on minimum Canadian content in terms that are not merely quantitative, but qualitative as well.

The criteria for quality programming might be difficult to establish, but the regulatory agency could begin with program budgets and go on to program philosophy. And any fool can tell the difference between "Gilligan's Island" and "A Gift To Last," or between a Miss Canada pageant and a National Geographic special. There is no doubt which of those programs panders to the lowest common denominator and which of them informs or stimulates.

Even if the technological revolution does not have the expected effect, and the CBC were able to continue as a microwave network, there ought to be a way to free it from the tyranny of numbers. In the United States, PBS's highest-rated programs draw about 5 per cent of the available American audience, and a show that consistently gets "a five" on commercial television is in trouble even in this country. In the United States, it's cut completely, very early in the schedule.

Yet PBS, which gets all its revenue from private donations and corporate and government grants, has been emboldened enough to ask Washington for more money. An increased PBS grant is being opposed on the grounds that it has an elitist audience, and that it is undemocratic to spend public funds on an operation that cannot make its own way in the marketplace. The critics ask whether it would be fair for PBS's predominantly upper-middle-class audience to be subsidized by the plain folk who prefer quiz shows.

Quite apart from the fact that the PBS audience probably pays as much tax as all of the people who like quiz shows, I think the answer is yes. Does the United States government maintain a splendid National Gallery in Washington because 220 million people are lined up to get in? Is the Library of Congress a waste of the taxpayers' money because the bulk of the citizenry doesn't use it?

In this country, we have a Canada Council, which is ignored or ridiculed by the newspapers and most of the citizenry. We have a National Film Board, which continues to make excellent films despite what would be a disastrous box office in commercial terms. Ballet is supported by governments, despite the multitude's conviction that it exists largely for the edification of capering faggots in long underwear. Governments support symphonies and art galleries and the theatre not because they are popular, but because they are unpopular, and couldn't survive without the public purse. Legislators do that because they realize that without them we would be a lesser nation. Whether the bulk of the populace takes direct advantage of those institutions or not, their existence improves the quality of their lives. Ballet and art and music help to make Canada a civilized state. We support arts and letters as a nation because it is right that we should. And if we give in to the thesis that only what is popular is good, then God help us.

Somehow we have got to break out of the revolving door of commercial television; that since trash sells best, all we can sell is trash. That least voiced, most often followed principle has made commercial television the senior partner in the wholesale destruction of taste. If the new satellite-cable combination enables us to break out, it will not be a moment too soon, because thoughtful people have been abandoning television in droves.

I flatly refuse to believe that serious information programming cannot also be entertainment, in the dictionary sense of the word. The shorter Oxford describes entertainment as "the action of occupying attention agreeably; that which affords interest or amusement." Those are terms with which the purest of successful documentary and news producers now live in reasonable comfort. In other words, we are not beaten before we begin by the nature of the medium. If the Gutenberg press had been used to give wider circulation to smut, it too would have been considered an invention of the devil.

Only a small percentage of the population of the United States reads the *New York Times*. It has been a stuffy and pretentious journal on occasion, a natural enough failing perhaps for any institution that has been the best for such a long time. But the standards of journalism it has espoused, not by lecturing people about them, but by teaching them through the power of daily example, has elevated the journalistic climate in the United States. It can be argued that without the *New York Times,* there would never have been a *Washington Post* or a *Los Angeles Times,* as we know them today. They now aspire to an excellence they hadn't dreamed of even two decades ago.

I think we could begin to correct what's wrong with television news in this country by establishing a distinguished national newscast. At the moment, the only organization which seems capable of that is the CBC. It becomes vitally important in my view that there be no final decision on a satellite network and Pay TV without a full discussion of the future role, operating philosophy, and financing of the CBC. The half-commercial, half-public concept isn't in anyone's interests.

If the CBC remains as a network, perhaps it is time to combine the Canadian experience with public TV and radio, and other similar institutions with the American experience in public broadcasting. If that part of the CBC budget which is now dependent on commercial revenue came instead from corporate and private donations, the schizophrenia would be cured. Once it was thrown out of the ratings game, the CBC could get on with the business of setting Canadian standards for television, particularly in news.

If Canada's three networks do disappear because of the revolution brewing in the south, then perhaps the CBC could become a satellite-cable operation, funded partly by a government grant, and partly by subscription to the CBC service, a form of Pay TV.

There will always have to be "popular" newscasts, newscasts that sell, as long as there is a mass market for news. And in their own way, because they are forced to communicate effectively to hold their audience – whether it is "the wad" or something better – they are necessary to the pursuit of excellence. But there should be one newscast in the country that is freed from the necessity of competing in the marketplace, from having to measure its success in terms of dollars and cents.

I'm thinking of a newscast which would deal not only with national and international political and economic news – and deal with those in a considered and analytical way – but a newscast which would give us the latest news on painting and the dance, music, sculpture, architecture, literature, film, ethnic cultures, archaeology, anthropology, history, science, agriculture, the environment, athletics as opposed to sports, and geography. A newscast of and about quality, to give Canadians a yardstick for achievement and for television news. At the moment, our newscasts barely mention the Order of Canada awards and the Canadians who win them, the Royal Bank of Canada's annual $50,000 award, or the Canada Council's grants and awards.

Such a newscast should not be heavy-handed or pedantic, as the CBC is now inclined to be when it finds itself on what it considers to be an elitist mission, but interested and inquiring. It should be prepared not by specialists, but by men and women with enough intellectual curiosity to read a little more widely than the papers and *Maclean's* magazine, people who are still capable of being excited by deeds and ideas. Such a newscast might even confound the experts by becoming popular. Even now, there is more room for quality than the programers suspect. They are losing viewers because they are programming for "the wad," and "the wad" alone.

Global's news budget continues to be hopelessly inadequate for a serious national news service, despite the fact that the new network has put more of its program budget into news than was reasonable in commercial terms. Several of us had to threaten to quit before we got any budget at all for covering the 1979 federal election, during another round of financial troubles that spring. Our executives were willing to listen, not because we could do anything to change the balance sheet, but because without its news service, Global would probably long before have gone under as a network. The news service has given us standing not just with the CRTC, but has generated prestige and credibility with viewers, advertisers, the banks, and the rest of the financial community. All of this convinces me that quality — which Global News achieves in patches — is a marketable commodity.

We have at least been trying to deal with the unmistakable signs of Canadian decay that have not been adequately dealt with by the rest of the medium. National television news tends to cover big government, big industry, big unions, big money, big interests, big disaster, big confrontation. And it covers human problems in terms of big statistics.

Somehow, if television news is to qualify as a daily national meeting-place, it must begin to do for the whole country what Global tried to do, and now only does sporadically, for southern Ontario. It must begin to rub shoulders with ordinary people and transmit their aspirations and their concerns, their basic decency to the leadership, which seems strangely out of touch with their views. Despite the fact that news tends to be bad, newscasts must try to become less destructively negative. They now tend to transmit complaints rather than encouragement, narrow-mindedness rather than liberality, events rather than thought. As a result, the national newscasts manage to convince the politicians that people are upset about rising fuel prices and impending shortages, but not that they're ready to support serious attempts to conserve fuel and develop new energy sources.

TV news must somehow come to grips with the issues that really affect people, and reflect them accurately. It isn't today's inflation that really worries Canadians, but what it will do to all of our tomorrows. Canadians are losing faith in the legal and educational systems, and their fellow citizens. English-speaking Canadians do not trust the French Canadians any more than the garage mechanic on the corner. We are fat and prosperous, and, in a starving, underdeveloped world, are slightly disgusted by our own bad health and affluence. As always, we are worried about the Americans, who now own most of our resources, not primarily because they're an acquisitive people, or even because you never give a sucker an even break, but because we were pathetically eager to sell them. Deep down inside, we know that and regret it, while we continue to stow our sense of adventure in an old sock under the mattress. We're confused about what we are, because we're becoming more and more American. In time, the Americans will own not just our resources but also our minds, because thanks to Canadian television, we are subletting our thought processes too. Canadians are worried about pollution and more fearful than they like to admit about the bomb.

I keep coming back to Harry Boyle, who late in 1975 talked to the *Toronto Sun*'s Sylvia Train about his years at the CBC.

"I don't really know why I stayed that length of time," he told her. "I do know I was thoroughly convinced that the radio network was the only unifying factor in the country... In the latter part, when I went into TV, I wanted to have a news magazine on the little events, the incidents that were happening all across the country – not the political or big happenings. I really couldn't convince the CBC of the merit of what I was trying to do and I finally felt I could do no more."

We still do not have Harry Boyle's national thermometer on network television. And we need it now much more desperately than when Harry Boyle left the CBC more than a decade ago. I still remember the promotional material that Global News cranked out before we went on the air, in which we promoted ourselves as an alternative service.

"We'll be showing a lot of things you don't expect on a television news program," one brochure said. "Traditional television has more to do with action than thought. It reports big disasters but never small triumphs. Our reporters are interested not just in how people suffer, but in how people live. People won't believe in the news, until news believes in people.''

So much for glib good intentions. We have tried to keep that promise in sight, despite recurring financial nightmares mixed wickedly with the great spoiler, audience acceptance. But we slip back to the tried and true – the official pronouncements from Ottawa and Washington, the oil fire, and murder trial, the horror story of the DC-10.

Much of television news will continue to be shallow and meaningless until the industry changes its mind about what the news is there for and what it's supposed to do. We will not be able to attract men and women of quality to sit in front of a television camera reading someone else's carefully sanitized words on everything from disaster to the weather in the same sprightly, carefully modulated tones. That's not a job for a journalist. It's a role.

If we had better people in television news, better informed, more aware of the stakes in the deadly game the world is playing, people who cared, we'd have better newscasts. We could begin to turn some of our weaknesses into freedoms, which ultimately are strengths.

One of the most widely recognized weaknesses, for example, is Walter Cronkite's horror of distortion through compression. The distortion occurs because the television newscasts try to duplicate not just the quantity but the kind of news that goes into the daily newspapers. Cronkite speaks of a hundred pounds of raw news, and a one-pound sack to put it in. We go through the tortures of compression only because we accept that the whole hundred pounds, ideally, should go on the air. But our obvious inability to put it all on the air should free us to be selective, free to concentrate on the news that ought to be covered, the news that affects our viewers most deeply.

Because we are nothing without an audience, and because television is a responsive medium, the best people in the business are more sensitive to the people they're addressing than most newspapermen. The TV newsman, the camera, and the transmitter, and thousands of people in their living rooms, are all locked together in the same illusion.

If we are well-informed and sensitive to the real feelings of our audience, we will be in a position to throw out ninety-eight or ninety-nine pounds of the Cronkite collection, or perhaps even the whole thing. We should feel free to decide ourselves what news is, without trying to impose the ancient yardsticks of print on a medium for which they were never intended.

We should begin to take risks. We might, for example, experiment with a two-pound, one-hour newscast that covered the conventional rip-and-read news on camera in the first five minutes. We would use the remaining forty-five minutes for a half-a-dozen, in-depth visual stories on the things that people were glad about or sad about that day, whether it was the murder of a Mountbatten, the continuing failure of the Toronto Maple Leafs, the imminence of Quebec's separation, the teenage suicide rate, government spending, solar heating, mortgage interest plans, some new Maggie Trudeau story, or a long-term shift in the weather. It would also give us a chance to pause for breath and put the more conventional national and international stories into perspective, at real turning points in the development of those stories, freeing us from trying to keep up with the contradictory, ongoing litany of governments and Prime Ministers. We might try using general reporters with several recognized areas of interest, rather than sports editors or business editors or weathermen.

I must admit that I am not as totally enamoured of the astonishing CBS success, ''60 Minutes,'' as some of my colleagues and some of my colleagues and some of the critics. I feel it has a tendency to use a sledge hammer, or Mike Wallace, on gnats, and that it avoids some of the most pressing issues altogether. It leans on the Afghanistan principle in its political coverage, and its best moments are often the lighter ones, with Morley Safer or Andy Rooney.

But it does not, as Braithwaite puts it, deal in consensus and shy away from all controversy. Its opinions, when delivered, are neither shallow nor meaningless. In June of 1978, ''60 Minutes'' did a highly critical report on the Ford Pinto, despite the fact that the show's principal sponsor at the time was the Ford Motor Company. It was not only a measure of courage, but a measure of the show's incredible success, that producer Don Hewitt was able to get away with it.

"60 Minutes" is a quality program, hosted by clever and experienced journalists. Mike Wallace, Morley Safer, Harry Reasoner, and Dan Rather are not good because they are stars, but stars because they are good, because they know their craft and its subtleties, because they have judgement and are not afraid of their own convictions. The astonishing thing, to the giant minds who programmed only for "the wad" is that "60 minutes" sells. As it headed into its twelfth season, recently, it was consistently in the top ten programs of the American ratings.

What that means is that the space salesmen are able to flog time in "60 Minutes" at rates as high as $215,000 per commercial minute. Since the hour is relatively cheap to produce – when compared to situation comedy or cop shows – it is also profitable. When you consider that the show's weekly budget is about the same as the rate for a single commercial minute, and that there are six commercial minutes in each show, you realize how profitable.

None of the competitors of "60 Minutes," despite the fact that they have lifted its format almost intact, have had the success of "60 Minutes, " either critically or commercially. The difference is in the quality of the people who produce, host, and otherwise put the competing shows to air. Without the right people, a format is just an empty frame.

There is a lesson in all of this for any Canadian network executive with the wit to see it, whether the future lies in satellites and cable or whether in Canada we hang on for a time to the old means of transmission. "60 Minutes," after all, had a Canadian antecedent, a runaway current affairs success that was also among the top ten programs in its marketplace. The program was "Seven Days," with Patrick Watson. Whether or not you agreed with the kind of journalism it practised, it proved that a quality information program could be sold. It was, for a time, a program that many Canadians felt they could ill-afford to miss. If you had gone to bed early on Sunday night, you were excluded from the conversation around the office water-cooler on Monday morning. It too made news, and it too was a program of opinion.

But it appears that the CBC bureaucracy is always the last to learn anything from its own revolutionaries. For too long, perhaps, they have remembered "Seven Days" not as an incredibly successful program, but as a monumental administrative problem.

Bill Cunningham came into my office, seething, one morning as I was putting some final touches on this book. A CBC news producer had just asked permission to come and have a look at our facilities, particularly the newsroom-studio combination, which is now so familiar to the audience in southern Ontario.

It is no secret that the CBC is now taking a hard look at our old-time slot, from 10:00 P.M. to 11:00 P.M., for a combination national news and newsmagazine program. It will be ironic if, when the CBC finally tries the time slot it should have occupied years ago, an hour in which first CTV and then Global cleared the land and cut the trees, it also does it from a newsroom that resembles Global's.

What made Cunningham angry on the morning in question is that there is nothing in our newsroom that he hadn't recommended to the CBC thirteen years earlier. And by now, some of it is becoming old-hat. Our newsroom-studio combination has already served as a model for the new CHAN-TV facilities in Vancouver, and is currently the inspiration for Ted Turner's new Cablenews operation in Atlanta.

"As soon as you leave," Cunningham remarked, "you're the expert. But because you fought too hard for those things while you were there, they'll never hire you again."

And so the CBC continues to pick the brains of the people who were too hot to handle – the Nolans, Watsons, Leitermans, Cunninghams – secure in the knowledge that none of them is petty or ungracious enough to refuse. But there is no money in it for them, and worse, very little satisfaction.

That is one of the reasons that, despite its many faults, I remain at Global. The new network realized from the beginning that a newscast that pulls no punches, that expresses opinions, that deals in people, is good business. Honesty is itself good business, in everything from using a real newsroom as a studio, or using working anchormen, to identifying U.S. network newsfilm. Honesty sells.

Oddly enough, the advertisers knew something about Global News even before the audience did. And although the newsroom and the network argue constantly about the interpretation of the figures, the news operation became self-supporting, to all intents and purposes, very early in the struggle – something of a Canadian first. It should not have been left to tiny Global to discover that the Canadian people have long been under-rated and sold short.

And it is not simply sins of omission that we're talking about. By feeding the audience Pablum, news that's easy to swallow, the Canadian networks have actively discouraged the growth of intellectual teeth.

I don't think it's any accident that commercial television is worse today, by almost any standard you care to apply, than it was ten years ago. Television, because of its enormous impact, tends to create what it portrays. TV itself, by pandering to the lowest common denominator, has debased North American standards to such a degree that before long, the people who want better television will have only each other to talk to.

For the new technology, the handwriting is on the wall. In the fall of 1979, a U.S. cable operator, Irving Kahn, warned his Canadian counterparts in Toronto that it would be suicidal for the new Canadian Pay TV industry if it offers anything but the best Hollywood movies and specials in the initial stages.

Kahn said he understood the concern in Canada about the social impact of American television. But he added that Pay TV must be highly attractive at the beginning if it's to be an economic success, and the only product with enough glitter is made in Hollywood, U.S.A.

For the government and the CRTC, the pressures from the industry are going to be enormous. Kahn wasn't telling the Canadian cable operators anything they didn't already know, or teaching them a battle song they weren't already singing.

How many Canadian parents have asked their children why they don't watch the "King of Kensington" or "A Gift To Last" and have heard the response: "Ah, gee, Dad, it's Canadian."

The trouble with the kind of branch plant communications industry we're running now is that all Canadian production, no matter what its merits, is seen more and more as second rate. The fact that it isn't second rate, or doesn't have to be, is obscured by our increasingly slick American tastes.

A lot of us, despite the benevolent brainwashing, remain Canadian. A lot of us, despite the Pablum, retain some intellectual curiosity. I suspect we're still in the majority, as a matter of fact, but we won't be the majority long because we're being starved to death.

We are, as I have suggested, on the brink of a television revolution, a revolution that could go either way. Quality television still has a chance in this country. But it is a chance that isn't going to come our way again.